GLASGOW
A Transport History

GLASGOW
A Transport History

MICHAEL MEIGHAN

AMBERLEY

For Tiago

First published 2024

Amberley Publishing
The Hill, Stroud
Gloucestershire, GL5 4EP

www.amberley-books.com

British Library Cataloguing in Publication Data.
A catalogue record for this book is available from the British Library.

ISBN 978 1 3981 1582 8 (print)
ISBN 978 1 3981 1583 5 (ebook)

Typeset in 10pt on 13pt Sabon.
Typesetting by SJmagic DESIGN SERVICES, India.
Printed in the UK.

Contents

Introduction

When I was a little boy living in Anderston, close to Central station and to the docks, Glasgow was one huge adventure playground for me. I would take my Ian Allan 'ABC' trainspotting book to any one of Glasgow's big terminal stations to record the steam locomotives coming and going. I could cross the Clyde on the Cheapside Street ferry and come back through the now abandoned Finnieston Tunnel. Or I could travel round the length of the rickety Glasgow Subway for pennies.

As Glasgow expanded and was redeveloped we saw huge changes in how we got around the city: paddle steamers and ferries disappeared from the Clyde; the Forth and Clyde Canal was closed and the Monklands Canal was replaced by the M8 Motorway; the horse and cart gave way to the petrol, then the diesel lorry; trams and trolleybuses were replaced by the bus; and steam locomotives gave way to electrification and to the 'blue train', which was to speed people into the city from the suburbs or newly built housing 'schemes' of Easterhouse, Drumchapel, Castlemilk and others.

Over the past few years the city has been reviewing how we get about. There are recently announced plans for a new metro and for new stations and connections. Railway lines are being expanded and electrified and the Subway is again being modernised. Arrangements for buses being taken back into public control have also just been announced, as has a new Active Travel Strategy for walking and cycling.

These new welcome developments affecting the greater Glasgow area led me to recall the many different methods of travel and transport that Glaswegians have experienced within the city and the huge changes that we have experienced. I hope you enjoy reading it as much as I have writing about it.

I have managed to obtain some excellent images. Every attempt has been made to seek permission for copyright material used in this book. However, if we have inadvertently used copyright material without permission, we apologise and will make the necessary correction at the first opportunity.

Michael Meighan

The Romance of the Clyde – Paddle Steamers, Puffers, Ferries and the Cluthas

It was the steam engine that changed sea travel and made faraway places accessible to travellers other than mariners. The same was true of the Scottish Highlands and Islands, much of it inaccessible then, and still is today, to a degree.

The islands were not the first to experience the sight of a steam-driven vessel, for that happened on one of Glasgow's canals, the Forth and Clyde. That first vessel was the *Charlotte Dundas*, named after Charlotte who was the daughter of a governor of the Forth and Clyde Canal, Sir Thomas Dundas.

William Symington and Patrick Miller of Dalswinton had been experimenting with a steam-powered boat that had travelled a small way on Dalswinton Loch, near Miller's house. Miller abandoned the project as costs were mounting but Symington continued with his work on engines and in 1800 Sir Thomas Dundas asked him to build a commercial steamboat to sail on the canal.

While apparently successful, there were fears that waves from the boat would damage the canal banks and so the *Charlotte Dundas* was abandoned at Lock 10 after serving many years as a dredger. It was an ignominious end to the project, but the idea was adopted by Henry Bell and it was not long before others adopted Symington's ideas and steam-powered canal boats began to appear. It was the beginning of steam navigation, an industry in which Glasgow and the Clyde were to excel over many years.

The Clyde Steamers

I remember one of my first experiences of sailing along the Clyde in the days when paddle steamers left from the Broomielaw to sail 'doon the water' to Dunoon, Ireland and other places on the way, including Govan, Greenock and piers along the Clyde.

My parents, brothers – one in my mother's arms – and I would line up with suitcases and prams to be helped up the gangplank at the Broomielaw onto the paddle steamer, which was a new experience, wonder and playground to a child. Just imagine, you could wander the ship, looking over the side to the great paddle wheels churning the black river water, or down to the engines, seeing the pistons working back and forth, amazed at the

Williamson-Buchanan's *Benmore* leaving the Broomielaw. (Michael Meighan Collection)

speed and power of the gleaming metal as the engineers travelled up and down with their rags and oil cans.

We would pass the tenements, the cranes, the ferries crossing and recrossing, the lines of ships moving in or out, to and from their worldwide destinations carrying all manner of goods such as whisky, jute and bananas. And then we would begin to see open fields. We would pass the imposing Dumbarton Rock and smell the brackish sea, a wondrous wide smell to accompany the whirling seagulls as we sailed on to a holiday at Innellan and new sea and country smells away from the smoke and grime of Glasgow.

The Clyde has a special place in Scottish maritime history. It was Henry Bell of Helensburgh who built *The Comet* in 1812 and started Europe's first passenger steamboat service, between Glasgow and Greenock. The boat was named after a comet that had been visible in the night sky during 1811–12. *The Comet* was advertised as sailing three times a week between Glasgow, Greenock and Helensburgh. Perhaps Bell was overambitious as the vessel was wrecked in heavy seas at Craignish Point during a service that had been introduced to Oban and Fort William.

Undaunted, a second boat was built, *Comet II*, but in 1825 she collided with the steamer *Ayr* at Gourock and sank, killing sixty-two passengers of the eighty on board.

The Broomielaw around 1876, with *Windsor Castle* centre. Also in the picture are *Balmoral,
Undine, Vesta, Eagle, Guinevere* and *Carrick Castle*. George Washington Wilson. (Michael
Meighan Collection)

Not surprisingly Bell gave up his interest in steam propulsion and while the rise of steam
navigation was meteoric, he derived no monetary benefit from his initiative. He was left
penniless but benefactors raised subscriptions on his behalf and the River Clyde Trustees,
in acknowledgement of his momentous invention, granted him an annuity of £100.00,
which was continued to his widow when he died in 1830.

Bell's invention was indeed momentous for within ten years there were around fifty
steamers on the Clyde, sailing down to Largs and up to Campbeltown and Inverary.

Incidentally it may have been Bell's hotel which gave rise to the expression 'doon the
water', for when he first introduced *The Comet*, one of the destinations was to his own Baths
Inn in Helensburgh where he and his wife, Margaret, invited visitors to 'take the waters'.

Another interesting fact that emerged from my research is that from 1864 most paddle
steamers on the Clyde were brand new, virtually all of the older ones having crossed the
Atlantic to North America. This was because during the American Civil War, shipowners
in Great Britain were easily enticed to sell their vessels to the Confederate States who were
using them to run the blockade that the Union side had set up outside the Confederate ports
of Charleston and Wilmington. Apparently Bermuda and Nassau were the centres of the
operation and while there were obvious dangers, the returns were such that a small number
of successful trips could clear the cost of the vessel and still provide a profit. One of these
was the CSS *Robert E. Lee* that had started life as the Glasgow to Belfast boat *Kangaroo*.

The *Kangaroo* was built in J. & G. Thomson's Clyde Bank Iron Shipyard in Govan for the J. & G. Burns Line. She was sold to the Confederate States Navy and was to become the most famous blockade runner before eventually being captured by the Union Navy and subsequently purchased by the Chilean Navy.

It is estimated that around 100 steamers left Great Britain and fifty of these were new ones built on the Clyde for the purpose. It is thought that this breaking of the embargo by supplying the Southern States with provisions and ammunition prolonged the Civil War by two years and therefore also delayed the end to slavery. This reflects badly on the Scottish attitudes to slavery in the United States, a history that has been exposed over recent years.

The Clyde fleet began to grow as Glasgow grew. As Glasgow expanded, the houses and factories did as well. The railways increased and so did the smoke, fog and grime, making life very difficult and uncomfortable for the residents. Steamers provided the getaway people needed. For the well-off came the opportunity to build fancy retreats along the river in places like Shandon, Kilcreggan and Innellan, well beyond the shipyards, to where they could commute daily or weekly to their new villas and mansions to escape the city. For the less well-off it was the opportunity to holiday, for at the Glasgow Fair holiday steamers would take them 'doon the water' to Dunoon, Rothesay and many other long-gone piers serving villages and towns all the way down the Clyde.

By 1900 there were around 300 steamers operating and this continued into the 1960s when cheap air travel made holidays in other countries, particularly Spain, possible.

One of the things that had originally helped increase the number of Glaswegians taking to the waves was the Temperance movement, which was instrumental in controlling alcohol in Scotland's growing industrial areas. In the mid-1800s drinking was out of control in a city that had 2,850 pubs, one for every fourteen citizens.

In 1853 the Forbes Mackenzie Act banned the sale of alcohol on Sundays and after 11 p.m. on weekdays. Exemptions were only for hotels serving meals to 'bona fide' travellers. As steamships in passage were exempt from the regulations, enterprising publicans were quick to see the opportunities. What is now called a 'booze cruise' became very popular and gave rise to the term 'steaming' for being extremely drunk.

As the popularity of the steamers grew, the continuing demand for speed in order to get ahead of the competition, even racing to be first at a pier, was creating some very fast vessels.

Side-wheeled paddle steamers as used on the Clyde developed rapidly due to their excellent maneuverability on the narrow reaches of the upper Clyde, congested as it was by shipping, as well as their ease in approaching the small piers. Their wide decks also afforded lots of space for travellers to marvel at the passing landscape.

While fascinating to watch, the method of powering paddle steamers was intrinsically inefficient. Paddle steamers were operated by reciprocating steam engines: steam generated by boilers drove pistons and the back and forwards movement of these pistons drove the paddle wheels. This constant momentum of large moving parts put strain on the engines, meaning they needed constant maintenance and repair.

This problem was solved in a way that transformed sea travel. The steam turbine was invented by Charles Parsons in 1884. It overcame the problems in paddle-driven vessels by having only rotating parts. While the Admiralty bought two vessels, HMS *Viper* and HMS *Cobra*, these naval vessels fitted with steam turbines were

Passengers enjoy a day trip to Kilcreggan on the PS *Waverley*. (Michael Meighan)

lost at sea through problems unrelated to the engines. This set back the use of the technology, as the Admiralty were not yet convinced that the engines would work to their satisfaction.

One gentleman was persuaded by a technical paper by Parsons and asked him about the possibility of using steam turbines to power merchant ships. This was Alexander Denny of William Denny and Brothers of Dumbarton. When invited by Denny to take on steam turbines, the railway operators were not interested in the concept. It took a private operator to take a risk and that was when a consortium including Captain John Williamson was formed with him saying that he would operate a steam turbine-powered ship for a season if one was built. Denny and Brothers then built the hull while Parsons Marine Steam Turbine Company built the engines. Each of the three partners, forming the Turbine Steamer Syndicate, contributed a third of the cost of the new ship, which was launched at Dumbarton on 16 May 1901.

It was a giant leap of faith but the TSS *King Edward* entered service on 1 July 1901 with daily sailings from Greenock to Dunoon and Rothesay, Fairlie, Lochranza and Campeltown. Returning to Greenock, passengers could take a train from the railway pier to arrive in St Enoch station at 6.18 p.m.

It was immediately successful and sailings on the Clyde entered a new phase that would take us into the 1960s. The launch of the TSS *King Edward* was followed by the TS *Queen Alexandra*, at which time the company became Turbine Steamers Ltd. The TS *Queen Mary* was launched at Denny's Dumbarton shipyard in 1933 for Williamson-Buchanan Steamers, which was the successor to Turbine Steamers. It was, at the time, the largest steamer on the Clyde. Berthed at the Bridge Wharf, it carried 13,000 passengers each week.

The TS *Queen Mary* has had an interesting career. In 1935 Cunard was preparing for the launch of their new transatlantic liner, which was soon to be launched by Her Majesty Queen Mary. Williamson-Buchanan was asked if they would change the name of their vessel to *Queen Mary II* to allow for the name to be used for the new liner.

H. le Bret and A. Bucquet, French passengers travelling to Inversnaid on Loch Lomond. (Michael Meighan Collection)

They graciously accepted. In 1976, following the removal of the RMS Queen Mary from Llloyd's Register, it was re-registered as TS *Queen Mary*.

The *King Edward* had proved Parsons, Denny and Williamson right and their enterprise revolutionised excursion cruisers, proving that higher speeds could be reached without the vibrations of the paddle steamer. New orders for steam turbine vessels appeared almost immediately, particularly for use on the Clyde and across the Irish Sea and the English Channel.

Williamson-Buchanan was by no means the only company to operate steamers. It was possibly the largest in its time but there were also smaller operators such as the Glasgow and Inverary Steamboat Company, which existed from 1909 to 1912 and operated the famous *Lord of the Isles*.

Among the new steamship operators were George and James Burns, who introduced a passenger steamboat service in 1821 between Glasgow and Ayr and later expanded to Liverpool and Belfast. George Burns was the co-founder along with Samuel Cunard and David McIver of the company that became the famous Cunard Steam-Ship Company. John Burns, George's son, became the chairman of the Cunard Line and 1st Baron Inverclyde. The Cunard Line prospered under his chairmanship and then of his son George A. Burns.

In 1851 the Burns brothers passed their Clyde and Hebridean fleet to David Hutcheson, who had worked for them. The new company was David Hutcheson & Co. The three partners were David Hutcheson, Alexander Hutcheson and David MacBrayne. In 1878 David MacBrayne took over the company and started what has become a shipping legend on the West Coast running services to the Clyde coast and most of the islands of the Inner and Outer Hebrides.

The family-run company got into financial difficulties in the 1920s and was bankrupt in 1928. Lack of a purchaser brought government intervention and the formation of a new company, David MacBrayne (1928). This was jointly owned by the London, Midland & Scottish Railway (LMS) and Coast Lines. This remained until 1969 when the Scottish Transport Group was formed, and took over the 50 per cent owned by Coast Lines. The LMS had already been nationalised and MacBrayne's now formed part of that project, merging with the Caledonian Steam Packet Company (CSP) to form Caledonian MacBrayne, still owned by the Scottish government. It is usually referred to as CalMac. It is now the largest operator of ferries in Great Britain, providing lifeline services to twenty-three West Coast islands and a number of routes in the Firth of Clyde. The ferries have black hulls and white superstructures and their funnels display a red Lion Rampant on their red funnels with black caps.

The Caledonian Steam Packet Company, with funnels painted yellow with a black top, had also been an early operator on the Clyde. It was started by the Caledonian Railway in 1888 to operate its steamers.

The Glasgow & South Western Railway Company and the London, Midland & Scottish (LMS) had also been running their own fleets, competing ferociously and dangerously with one another. This changed dramatically in 1923 when these fleets were merged with the Caledonian Steam Packet Company fleet.

Meanwhile the North British Railway became part of the London & North Eastern Railway (LNER) and this became part of British Railways under nationalisation in 1948. At the end of 1968 the CSP also passed to the Scottish Transport Group and in 1973 it gained control of most of David MacBrayne Ltd, becoming Caledonian MacBrayne.

Because of European legislation, the CalMac services were split and put out to competitive tender in 2006. A reactivated David MacBrayne Ltd won the tender and in 2016 they were again awarded the contract and now operate as Caledonian MacBrayne, shortened to CalMac.

Ships no longer sail from the Broomielaw, so the only way you could possibly imagine what it might be like to travel on the Clyde steamers would be to take an excursion on the PS *Waverley*, the last ocean-going paddle steamer in the world. Based in Glasgow, it is owned by the Paddle Steamer Preservation Society.

Named after Sir Walter Scott's first novel, the PS *Waverley* was built on the Clyde in 1946 for the London & North Eastern Railway Company (LNER) at a time when many of the larger railway companies ran their own steamers to connect with their rail services. The restored *Waverley* now sails in British waters from April till October. It is an absolute joy to sail on it on one of its trips on the Clyde.

You may also be able to sail on another iconic Clyde ship, for the TS *Queen Mary* has returned to the river. When it was retired from service it was sold to Glasgow District Council for conversion to a museum. Lack of funds stopped the project and it was sold on to a number of owners before languishing at Tilbury under threat of scrapping. The Friends of TS *Queen Mary*, funded by Glasgow businessman Jim McColl, purchased the ship at auction in 2015. Subsequent fundraising allowed necessary repairs before it

TS *Queen Mary* in the James Watt Dock, Greenock, after repairs in the Garvel dry dock. (dave souza, CC BY-SA 4.0 <https://creativecommons.org/licenses/by-sa/4.0>, via Wikimedia Commons)

arrived back on the Clyde where it is berthed at the Pacific Dock. It is due to return to passenger service in 2024.

I have mentioned in other places the contributions that Glasgow people made during the First and Second World Wars. This is true of the paddle steamers and the many coasters and fishing boats that were called into service during the wars as well as the brave crew who manned them. The predecessor to the present *Waverley* was also the PS *Waverley*. It was built in 1899 for the North British Steam Packet Co. and sailed on the Clyde until 1939 when it was requisitioned by the Admiralty and served as a minesweeper during both wars until it was sunk by a mine while assisting in the 1940 Dunkirk evacuation. Over 400 troops and some crew were lost while 285 survivors were picked up by another Clyde paddle steamer, the PS *Golden Eagle*, and more by other vessels.

The Puffers and the VICs

On either bank of the Clyde and on the islands grew small communities, and as they were often without piers or harbours they could only be served from the sea. This gave rise to the famous 'puffers' humorously immortalised in Neil Munro's *Para Handy Tales*.

While the *Charlotte Dundas* was not up to the job, the first practical steamboat was designed for canal work. The *Thomas*, built in 1856, was an iron boat with a simple steam engine without a condenser. Once the steam had powered the engine it was exhausted up the funnel in puffs – hence the familiar name 'puffer'. Even when condensers were fitted to later vessels, reusing the steam, the name stuck.

Three types of puffer emerged from this basic design. The 'inside' boats worked the canals while the 'shorehead' boats worked the Clyde from Glasgow as far as Bute and Loch Fyne. The 'outside' boats were longer but built for heavier seas out to the Hebrides. These three types of craft, both in their crewing and building, created a great deal of employment: there were twenty builders in Scotland with a high percentage around Kirkintilloch and Maryhill on the Forth and Clyde Canal.

As with many other vessels, the puffers were called into active service during the wars, particularly at Scapa Flow in Orkney, servicing the Home Fleet in the First World War. During the Second World War they were again called into action but this time as VICs – Victualling Inshore Craft. In 1939 the Admiralty placed orders for these craft and some of them entered civilian service back in the Clyde.

While the puffers had originally been steam driven, following the war, existing ones were often converted to diesel and continued to compete with road haulage. While the government subsidised the haulage of cargos to the islands, some operators found the subsidies impossible to work with. In addition, the use of roll-on roll-off ferries with new custom-built piers was increasing direct access to the islands and remote peninsulas for lorries carrying, for example, malt and casks to distilleries and whisky to Glasgow. The need for coastal vessels died out, and while larger vessels continued to carry bulk materials, the age of the puffers slowly came to an end to be survived by one or two remaining vessels entertaining tourists: VIC *32* at Crinan and MV *Spartan* at the Linthouse site of the Scottish Maritime Museum in Irvine. That's a great day out.

Clyde Ferry No. 8 discontinued in 1980. (Courtesy of gillfoto, CC BY-SA 4.0)

The Clyde Ferries

Almost as well loved as our trams were the Clyde ferries, those little vessels that crossed the Clyde at its narrowest within the city. They had two small covered areas either side of a small engine house, and at either end, a pilot's cabin next to the open gangways. I loved going down to the bottom of Clydeferry Street at night waiting for them to come into the landing through the thick river fog. The access steps were within one of the quayside warehouses and were barred on either side by high railings. It was quite spooky in there with the light of one electric bulb hardly illuminating the cobbled area as the wee ferry came slowly out of the dark of the river.

I loved those ferries from the very first moment my father took me on one. By day, sometimes on my travels I would go down and watch them come into the landing and up 'the bumps', for the landing was actually a set of large steps that the ferry would bump up against and people would jump off as soon as it touched. It was quite fun if it was a quiet day and you were allowed to go back and forwards across the river.

At one time there was huge industry on both sides of the Clyde and the ferries would be packed with workers coming and going to the shipyards, factories and warehouses. Crossing the river could be a hazardous occupation as the river got busier and shipbuilding increased along the banks. The inevitable happened in 1864 when a rowing ferry carrying twenty-seven men from Clyde Street, Anderston, to Springfield Quay was swamped by the swell of a passing steamer. Only eight were saved from the freezing water. Two of

The Finnieston
vehicle ferry crossing
the river in a typical
Glasgow fog. In
the distance is the
North Rotunda of
the original Clyde
Tunnel. (Michael
Meighan Collection)

these were rescued by the ferryman at the Hyde Park Ferry further along the river. They
had clung to the boat as it was carried downstream. This accident was to precipitate
the introduction of steam ferries in 1865. By 1900 there were ten ferries serving seven
landings, around a quarter of a mile apart.

In 1878 the Clyde Navigation Trust was granted permission to operate a vehicular
ferry and sought a design that would suit all tide conditions and which would not impede
other traffic. The solution was provided by Wm Simons & Co. in 1890. The new ferry,
The Finnieston, also known as the *Horse Ferry*, had a steam-operated lifting deck that
could move to suit tide conditions, and being double-ended, with twin screws at either
end, it was highly manoeuvrable and did not need to turn in the river.

The ferry could carry up to eight carts and 300 passengers from Mavisbank Quay on
the south side to Finnieston on the north. It was successful right away and was followed
by a second one in 1905 at Whiteinch and in 1912 the old chain ferry at Govan was
replaced by another. The Finnieston crossing was discontinued in 1966; the Clyde Tunnel
had been opened in 1963 and the ferry was largely redundant.

By the way, it was Simons shipyard in Renfrew which provided the *Corozal*, a dredger
that carried out major excavation work on the Panama Canal. Simons specialised in
dredgers and the *Corozal* was the most powerful dredger ever to be built. The story of
Simons is told in Paisley Museum.

The Yoker, or most commonly known as the Renfrew Ferry, looking from the south bank. Once a chain-pulled vehicle crossing, it is now operated using a fast pedestrian ferry.

The Cluthas

While the steamers were designed for longer journeys along the Clyde, the Cluthas (Clutha comes from the Romans or early Britons) were another type of vessel. They were smaller and acted as river buses, plying from the Victoria Bridge up the river to Linthouse. The full trip would cost you one penny and take forty-five minutes and cover 3 miles and eleven landing stages. It was cheap, except that with slatted wooden seats, the journey could be quite uncomfortable, particularly if you were forced to stand or sit on deck. Given that the weather could be very inclement, I would assume that the lounge below might not be very comfortable either.

The idea of a river service was proposed in the 1870s as an alternative to horse-drawn buses. The services started in 1884 and by 1896 there were twelve vessels titled simply *No 1* to *No 12*. By the mid-1890s they were carrying 2 to 3 million passengers per year.

In 1898, electric tramcars were introduced and the resulting speedier service and faster journeys meant that besides the railway, there was additional competition. It was the beginning of the end for the river service. They were discontinued in 1903, being dispersed throughout Great Britain. *No 1* continued as a messenger boat till 1924 and *No 4*, renamed *The Comet*, was kept as a launch for visitors and staff. It was scrapped in 1946.

Clutha No. 6. (Michael Meighan Collection)

Clutha landing at the bottom of Jamaica Street. (Michael Meighan Collection)

The Railway Network
Around Glasgow

Some of my earliest and strongest memories are of steam trains. While I must have been aware of our busy roads full of horses and carts, trams and motor cars, it was seeing my first steam locomotive when I was very young that made such a lasting impression and helped create a lifelong interest in railways.

I must have been around five years old when I was first introduced to the power of steam. We were on one of our outings to Balloch or Helensburgh where my parents would take us on picnics to the beaches. We stayed at the bottom of North Street, in a tenement now long

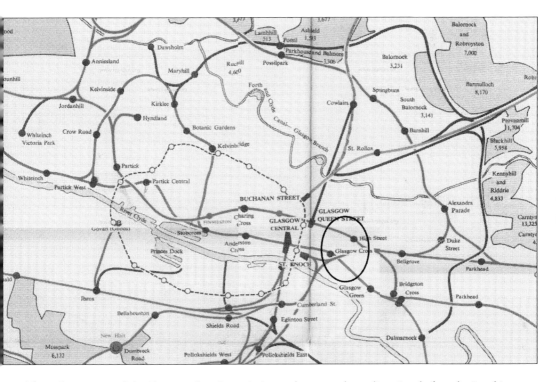

The railway network in Glasgow showing existing and proposed new lines just before the Beeching Axe. (Michael Meighan Collection)

gone, to be replaced by the concrete supports for the Kingston Bridge. From there we would walk up to the old Charing Cross station and into the ticket office, into that irreplaceable smell of old wood, smoked from years of steam locomotives passing underneath. For this was an era before plastics, when everything was made of wood, leather, iron and brass.

Down below were the platforms and there I stood, sheltering beneath my father's arms as the thundering noise emerged from that dark recess at the end of the platform. All at once, the iron monster emerged at speed, in a cloud of steam and smoke. There was a horrendous noise of screeching brakes and then a great slamming of doors as passengers decanted and we two wee boys were ushered into one of the train doors. This of course was the beginning of yet another wonder as, with a whistle from the platform, and a great puffing from the locomotive, the train entered the tunnel at the other end of the platform and plunged us into a world of darkness lit only by a faint light from the ceiling above us in this little compartment. This was a time when there were few corridor trains and the compartment was simply a room with a long upholstered bench at either side and a door at each end, on which there was a window held open or closed by pulling up or down on a long leather strap with holes in it, just like a thick trouser belt. The belt holes would slot into a brass peg to hold the window open.

We had very little time to be fearful of this dark tunnel, for in no time at all we were into the sun as the train climbed out of the tunnels to emerge at Yorkhill, next stop Partickhill, and we were on our way out of the city on what was the original City & District Railway.

Sailors boarding a train in Glasgow Central station. (Michael Meighan Collection)

It was the North British Railway that was instrumental in building this line. Queen Street station was becoming congested as rail traffic increased. After consideration of a new terminal station in the west of Glasgow, it was decided to build a new line with a four-platform station underneath the existing Queen Street station.

Much of the 3-mile length from College station on the High Street to Stobcross was built using the 'cut and cover' method in which giant trenches were opened and the line built quite near the surface.

The Glasgow City & District Railway was opened in March 1886 and was a roaring success, immediately taking traffic from Queen Street station and allowing through traffic from east to west. This connection of short line to short line was typical in the development of Scotland's railways. The original tracks were built by landowners and business people and were designed mostly for moving coal and other minerals from mines to towns, factories and harbours. When it came to building longer railways to connect towns and cities, the developers had major problems. They had to negotiate with owners of short lines and even canal companies in order to get their lines built. It was only the strong that survived through merger and acquisition, or line sharing agreements.

Typical of these was the Garnkirk & Glasgow Railway, which was incorporated in 1826 and eventually ran from Coatbridge to Townhead. The route turned out to be a convenient one for the Caledonian Railway to use when they expanded in 1854. It had originally been promoted by Charles Tennant & Co., who owned the St Rollox Chemical Works in Townhead, and was built mainly to break the monopoly in supply of coal held by Glasgow coal mine owners and by the Monklands Canal Company. Before the First World War there were around 120 individual railway companies, mostly making losses and in competition with one another. During the war these were brought together under state control, which lasted until 1921. While full nationalisation was then considered, the solution adopted was one designed to minimise competition while maintaining some of the economies of scale found during the war. The Railways Act of 1921 brought together most companies in a grouping that resulted in the London & North Eastern Railway (LNER), the London, Midland & Scottish (LMS), the Great Western Railway (GWR), and the Southern Railway (SR). It was *Railway Magazine* that gave them the name 'Big Four'. Everything before 1 January 1923 is known as 'Pre-grouping'.

Full nationalisation was achieved by the government following the Second World War, when the Transport Act of 1947 formed British Railways (BR). This tenure of British Railways saw a massive changeover from steam locomotives to diesel and electric, and a move away from freight to passengers. It also saw the reduction of 30 per cent of the railway network in the 1960s. It was renamed British Rail in 1965 and would remain so until railway privatization took place between 1994 and 1997.

By the 1950s, rail lines criss-crossed Glasgow with stations as numerous as the London Underground. We also had terminal stations at Maryhill, Bridgeton, Gallowgate, Partick and Hyndland.

Hyndland, for example, serviced the fine buildings of the new leafy suburban West End. The line was opened by the North British Railway Company in 1886 with a link to the Stobcross line. It terminated in an elegant two-storey building with a long platform and an iron and glass canopy. Thirty trains a day used the station, travelling to Airdrie or Hamilton, and there had even been services direct from King's Cross, London, to Glasgow (Hyndland). As with many stations it also had a goods and coal yard. All are gone now save a little park, 'Old Station Park', opened in 1985.

Coal was the heaviest and the most needed commodity by residents in Glasgow and this came into the city by train to be dispersed to numerous local goods yards like Hyndland and Partick. Workers travelled back and forth to the huge factories, including the giant Singer sewing machine factory at Clydebank, which had a special station built for it. Walter McFarlane's great Saracen Iron Works was based in Possil and a station was built there to accommodate the influx of workers. The same was true of the long-closed Glasgow Green station, which served the huge Templeton's carpet factories and the textile mills in the east end. The now partially closed Lanarkshire & Dumbartonshire Railway served the shipyards and factories burgeoning along the banks of the Clyde as well as the 'new town' of Clydebank and it connected to the growing town of Helensburgh and townships along the lower Clyde. Many of these railway tracks have now become walkways and cycle ways. Among these is the Glasgow Central Railway that was built in stages from 1894 and allowed the Caledonian Railway to access the docks and factories on the north of the Clyde.

While railways served the docks all along the Clyde, the greatest development was the General Terminus and Glasgow Harbour Railway, which was to come into its own with the development of the Ravenscraig integrated steel mills. First opened in 1848, its role was to provide a link and a facility for the movement of coal from the Lanarkshire and Ayrshire coalfields to the Clyde. In 1954 the Terminus saw a new lease of life as it was a perfect location for the 12,000-ton ships arriving to deliver iron ore for the steelworks in Motherwell. In 1954 1.5 million tons of ore from Sweden, Newfoundland and north Africa were offloaded.

I lived in Anderston in the 1950s and I saw the huge iron ore cranes built. I also saw them demolished in the 1980s with the opening of the Hunterston Terminal in North Ayrshire. I often watched the offloading as the ore was dumped by the cranes in the midst of great clouds of 'stoor'. The ore was then transported to Ravenscraig via the Glasgow Harbour Railway. The railway, General Terminus Quay and the ore handlers have now all disappeared, replaced by business parks and housing.

I was particularly familiar with the Glasgow Central Railway, which ran in tunnels under the city, and can confirm the criticisms that the stations were dark and smoky, for my father would take me by train, possibly football specials, to Parkhead for Celtic matches or Rutherglen to see Clyde playing. That would probably have been from Anderston Cross station.

During my first year at secondary school I even took the steam train to school, from Charing Cross to High Street. That was short-lived for that was when the railway was closed for modernisation and it would be a few years before I was to travel that route again. By that time, in 1960, it had been transformed into a new, comfortable and fast service with brand-new Electric Multiple Units (EMUs) which became known as the Blue Trains. I remember the very first time on one of these when my father took us to see our new house in Knightswood, not far from Scotstounhill station.

R. M. Casserley has captured the claustrophobic atmosphere in Central station low level in 1957. (R. M. Casserley)

I was to get used to those trains when I started my apprenticeship in Coatbridge near the other end of the line. The trains were extremely comfortable and warm. These three-car sets, Class 303, built by the Pressed Steel Company in Linwood, Paisley, were considered to be the best multiple units ever built and I can certainly testify to their comfort as, having to get up at around 6.00 a.m. to start my journey, I was often fast asleep and carrying on to Airdrie at the end of the line.

'Blue Train' 303031 to Wemyss Bay on the Inverclyde Line, at Glasgow Central station. (Michael Meighan Collection)

Airdrie was then the eastern end of the new North Clyde Line that ran from there to Helensburgh and Balloch via either Yoker or Singer. It also ran on a separate line from Westerton to Bearsden, Hillfoot and Milngavie.

British Railways 1955 Modernisation Plan

All of this revolution in travel was the product of the British Railways 1955 Modernisation Plan that was designed to tackle the loss of traffic and revenue to airlines and roads by upgrading the railways, making them safer, faster, more efficient and more cost-effective.

The eventual success of this project was debatable but one of the objectives was the electrification of certain main lines, the completion of which certainly improved Glasgow's passenger network, giving us the North Clyde Line and the other electrified line, the Cathcart Circle.

While the electrification of these lines was successful, the attempt to stem losses in the railways was a failure in many ways. While British Railways' plans for Glasgow were for further electrification of other lines and the introduction of diesel locomotives, the Macmillan government of 1959–63 had other ideas. Frustrated at the apparent mismanagement of railways and continued reduced traffic, they commissioned Dr Beeching to report on *The Reshaping of British Railways*. The report, produced in 1963, and the implementation of which was termed the 'Beeching Axe', led to the closure of 2,400 stations and thousands of miles of track. In Glasgow this included the line along the Clyde paralleling the North Clyde Line and which is now open as part of the long-distance path, the Clyde Walkway.

The UK government was not the only body wielding the axe at that time. In 1945 a report by Robert Bruce, the Glasgow Corporation Engineer, was instrumental in the wholesale redesign of Glasgow city centre. His *First Planning Report to the Highways and Planning Committee of the Corporation of the City of Glasgow* was the basis of twenty Comprehensive Development Area (CDA) plans which were to radically change the face of the city, creating industrial areas while demolishing tenements and moving residents from the city centre. The most drastic of these can be seen in Townhead and my own Anderston.

The plans also included the demolishing of a number of Glasgow's iconic buildings. Astonishingly these included the Glasgow School of Art and the Glasgow City Chambers. Luckily, good sense prevailed and while many precious buildings disappeared we kept those two. We also kept Glasgow Central and Queen Street stations, both of which had been destined for demolition.

Bruce's intention was that the four main Victorian railway stations would disappear and be replaced by Glasgow North and Glasgow South stations. Glasgow North was to be where the Old Buchanan Street station was, replacing both Queen Street and Buchanan Street stations. Glasgow South was to be roughly where Glasgow Central is, replacing it and St Enoch.

While these plans were never carried out, the 'Beeching Axe' did fall on the imposing St Enoch station, which was closed in 1966 with the hotel being demolished in 1977 amidst protests. A shopping centre and car park replaced the station and hotel. The less imposing Buchanan Street station closed in 1966 and was replaced by an office block.

The Glasgow Terminal Stations

It may seem strange that while Central station is now Glasgow's main railway terminal, it wasn't always so. Until Glasgow Central and St Enoch were opened, Glasgow's main terminal for southbound trains was at Bridge Street, on the other side of the river.

Bridge Street station, opened for traffic in 1840, was the terminal of the Glasgow & Paisley Joint Railway and became popular, particularly for those passengers used to the much longer steamer journeys from the Broomielaw down the Firth of Clyde to Greenock, Port Glasgow and beyond.

While we are familiar today with the plethora of different operating companies, it was much the same in the early days, before the grouping of railways under the Railways Act of 1921 and eventual nationalisation under the Transport Act of 1947.

Bridge Street station had been jointly managed by the Glasgow, Paisley, Kilmarnock & Ayrshire (GPK&AR) and the Glasgow, Paisley & Greenock (GP&G) railway companies and following mergers, the joint operators became the Caledonian Railway and the Glasgow & South Western Railway. For thirty years the station served their needs.

Bridge Street station of the Glasgow & Paisley Joint Railway. (Blyth and Blyth)

However, both companies wanted to get across the river, into the heart of the booming city, as well as link up with the expanding rail network north of the river.

Bridge Street station was on the south bank and the Clyde was a major obstacle. Crossing the Clyde was never going to be easy – even in entrepreneurial Victorian times when coal and the railways reigned supreme – as the Clyde Navigation Trust had something to say about any proposed bridges. While that end of the Clyde may be quiet now, at that time it was a bustling thoroughfare, and crossing it would have restricted trade up and down the river. Additionally, the existing road bridges provided profitable tolls and the owners objected to the competition from rail.

The first to overcome this obstacle was the City of Glasgow Union Railway, which was a joint enterprise between the G&SWR and the North British Railway. Their new Clyde Bridge, opened in 1870 and still standing, allowed traffic from the south across the river and gave access to all other directions via a bypass as well as to the new but temporary Dunlop Street station. The year 1876 was to see the opening of the new St Enoch station with four daily services to the Midland Railway's St Pancras station in London. Increase in traffic then saw the station expand with through services introduced from Edinburgh to Greenock, Ayr and Ardossan to connect with railway steamers. The prestigious St Enoch Hotel was to open three years later.

The hotel had actually been built by the City of Glasgow Union Railway but was acquired in 1883 by the Glasgow & South Western. St Enoch's was the city's largest hotel, with 200 rooms, and along with the station was the first building in Glasgow to be lit by electricity. St Enoch station suffered the same fate as many other routes and stations under Dr Beeching's railway rationalisation programme and closed in 1966. The hotel limped on for a number of years, but times and poor fire precautions caused its closure by British Railways in 1977. In the face of fierce protest from Glaswegians it was demolished.

The Clyde Bridge was extremely important, not just because it gave access to the station for passengers, but because it allowed a huge increase in freight traffic in all directions as well as the huge College goods yard which once stood at the corner of High Street and Duke Street. Glaswegians in the 1960s and '70s would have been very familiar with the iconic British Railways Scammell Scarab articulated trucks with three-wheel cabs that would come and go from the yards onto High Street.

You would have thought it sensible for both 'operating companies' to collaborate on both a crossing and a terminal, but it was not to be. There had been a certain amount of acrimony in jointly operating Bridge Street and this carried on. The 'Caley' thought that the G&SWR wanted too much for use of the proposed new station and bridge, so they decided to build their own, with plans drawn up in 1866 for a station at Gordon Street in the heart of the city.

It was not until August 1879 that trains finally departed the platforms at Gordon Street, renamed Central station. This was after the completion of the station buildings and the construction of the Caledonian Railway Bridge over the Clyde, designed by Blyth & Cunningham and built by Sir William Arrol. The crossing of the Clyde came at a cost to the Caley as the Clyde Navigation Trustees were putting up a fight. It cost £95,000 in compensation as well as ensuring that the piers of the new bridge were in line with the piers of the Jamaica Bridge to allow unhindered navigation.

The building of Glasgow Central station. On the right is Hope Street still with St Columba's 'Highland Cathedral' at the bottom. (Blyth and Blyth)

Caledonian Railway Bridge with St Enoch Hotel in the background. (Blyth and Blyth)

The bridge was built between 1876 and 1878 and there might have been some concerns given that the Tay Bridge Disaster occurred soon after. During a violent storm on 28 December 1879, the bridge, designed by Sir Thomas Bouch, collapsed while a train from Wormit to Dundee was passing over. The train went into the Tay and all on board were killed. The disaster was blamed on a number of things, including the lack of provision for wind loading and the quality of castings. Bouch had also submitted a design for the new Forth rail crossing but, unsurprisingly, the design wasn't used. The building of the Forth Bridge showed the advances in metallurgy and engineering over a short period of time as the bridge was the first structure in the world to be built entirely of steel. As the Forth Rail Bridge had also been built by Sir William Arrol there were obviously no concerns about quality and reputation with his new Central Station Viaduct.

From 1899 to 1905 the station was substantially extended to give thirteen platforms. The new work was designed by architect J. Miller and engineer Donald Matheson, with the steelwork being erected by the Motherwell Bridge & Engineering Co. This resulted in the familiar façade in Hope Street along with new platforms extending over Argyle Street. At the same time as the station was enlarged, a new bridge was constructed and came into use in 1905. It is a massive structure of steel set on solid granite piers. It was designed by Matheson and again built by Sir William Arrol. At the same time the older bridge was re-floored and strengthened. It survived to be demolished between 1966 and 1967. It was at the end of its life and new signaling systems had made the new viaduct more efficient.

This is a Fowler 4P, built at Derby in 1933. Advertisements were once a common feature of railway stations. (R. M. Casserley)

With the redeveloped Central station, it was felt that there was no need for Bridge Street station and it closed in 1905. From then, Glasgow Central station remained mostly unaltered until its part-renovation in the 1980s. A new five-year renovation programme started in 1998. The station was re-roofed and the building cleaned, making the huge station feel light and airy. With increase in passenger traffic two new platforms were also built.

Following the success of visits during a Doors Open day in 2013, regular station tours were introduced taking visitors into the huge undercroft containing workshops and storage. There are plans to open up a long-unused platform and install vintage rolling stock as well as a recreated bookstall and vending machine taking the visitor back to Victorian times.

Queen Street Station

Queen Street, Glasgow's other main terminal station, was built by the Edinburgh & Glasgow Railway in 1842. With the rearrangement of companies, the E&GR was absorbed into the North British Railway in 1865 and in 1923 this became part of the London & North Eastern Railway.

The building of the Cowlairs Tunnel to take trains from the centre of Glasgow underground up to Springburn was a major engineering accomplishment. However, the idea of putting a station into the heart of a city through a tunnel with only two running

The uniformed lads are Post Office telegraph boys. Queen Street station was just across the square from the General Post Office. (Michael Meighan Collection)

lines was a problematic chicken coming home to roost. Then, as now, the capacity of the station was limited by the width of the tunnel and the finite number of platforms available. The gradient through the tunnel was originally so steep that early steam locomotives couldn't manage it. Until 1909, when banking (additional) engines were introduced, trains had to be hauled up on a cable attached to a stationary engine that was situated beside Cowlairs station, which closed in 1964. In order to slow trains down approaching the station, a braking van was used.

Today's diesels have no problems with the gradient but there were operating difficulties in 1966 when Buchanan Street station closed as part of the 'Beeching Axe'. From then, the services to Aberdeen, Dundee and other destinations transferred to Queen Street. The problem was that the station is in a very confined space with a very small distance between platforms and the tunnel entrance. Now, ScotRail operates the trains, which have no problems managing the platforms and the gradient, although any problems or delays can still lead to bottlenecks.

Mentioned before was Queen Street Low Level opened in 1842 as the Glasgow terminus of the Edinburgh & Glasgow Railway with services reaching as far as Edinburgh Waverley. When Glasgow Central Low Level closed in 1964 it became the sole east-west line through the city until the reopening of the Central Low Level in 1979.

The Return of the Train

We are in a new railway age and while Glasgow has made mistakes in a love affair with the car driven through the heart of the city, it has come back to the train. The continually expanding network is well used and even loved by the Glaswegian. I was a young passenger on the new electric 'Blue Train' as it took its place in railway history, linking Airdrie to Milngavie, Helensburgh and Balloch. While Glaswegians had used the steam train for day trips to Balloch, the Blue Train made travel attractive and comfortable.

Perhaps the most welcome comeback, and one demanded by Glaswegians for many years, was the reopening of the Glasgow Central Railway tunnels. Closed under the Beeching Axe in 1965, the tunnels reopened in 1979 to join the North Clyde services to Lanark. As part of this, Argyle Street station was opened and another new one, on the site of the old Finnieston station, became Exhibition Centre to serve the new Scottish Exhibition and Conference Centre.

The Glasgow railway infrastructure is such that we can we can now travel from Helensburgh, Balloch and Milngavie through the city directly to Edinburgh Waverley on the reopened Bathgate line, which was joined to Airdrie in 2010. I take it often through the once heavily industrialised Lanarkshire countryside. If I wanted to go into town I can now also travel from Anniesland through Maryhill and Possilpark to Queen Street. That was a welcome surprise to me.

There are ongoing developments in the Glasgow area, one being the full electrification of the Barrhead to Glasgow line, a first phase in a programme of decarbonisation producing longer, greener and quieter trains between Barrhead and Glasgow. A similar development has been approved on the East Kilbride to Glasgow line.

However, given the size of the travelling population in Glasgow there are some glaring omissions that pressure groups are urging to be corrected. The first is the completion of the Glasgow Central to Glasgow Airport direct link that was cancelled in 2009 as part of public spending cuts. This would allow four direct trains per hour to the airport and remove an enormous amount of bus journeys as well as encourage more people to leave their cars at home. As part of the Edinburgh Glasgow Improvement Programme, Glasgow Queen Street station has also been modernised giving us a contemporary and accessible building with much-needed extended platforms.

Many people travelling from the south and heading to the north and to the east will know the difficulty in doing this as they have to make their way from Glasgow Central to Queen Street through the busy city centre or use the shuttle bus. A proposed Crossrail envisages reopening the City Union Line to connect the North Clyde to the Ayrshire and other lines south of the city. The initiative would see new or re-sited stations. High Street would move east to meet a newly electrified City Union Line. There would be a new Glasgow Cross station at the site of the Gallowgate station behind the Mercat Building. This would provide a link to the Argyle Line below. Cumberland Street station would be reopened and West Street Subway station enlarged and to provide a link to the railway. The oval on the railway map shows where this would be likely to happen.

Privatisation and Nationalisation

I mentioned earlier that the railways had been under state control since 1948, before which they had been run by the 'Big Four' railway companies. In 1994 the Conservative government decided that they would return the railways to private hands; ownership of the track would be by Railtrack and there would be twenty-five franchisees or Operating Companies for passenger transport while freight carrying would be sold in its entirety. The arguments for privatisation are that it brings improved services, reduced costs and is less of a burden on the taxpayer. There is a general agreement that the idea of having separate operating companies from those owning the track was misconceived. The idea was to copy the aircraft industry, which has aircraft owners but separate ground infrastructure. It was a simplistic idea based on an entirely different industry and never really worked. A major crash at Hatfield in England precipitated the eventual closure of Railtrack and its replacement by Network Rail, which still separately manages the railway infrastructure in Scotland.

Rail franchising effectively died and was removed in May 2021 when the rail system was partially re-nationalised. Because of the failure of the model, of the original franchisees, a number of them, the Caledonian Sleeper, LNER, Northern Trains, Southeastern and the Transpenine Express, are effectively in public ownership. Transport for Wales rail is now owned by the Welsh government. For some time in Scotland there had been pressure from the public to take Scottish railways back into public hands from the franchisee Abellio, which was considered to be underperforming. This was achieved when ScotRail became ScotRail Trains on 1 April 2022.

The future is presently uncertain in Scotland, for the UK government recently announced an Integrated Rail Plan (IRP) under which rail operations in Great Britain would be brought together under the state-operated public body Great British Railways, with operations on a concessions basis. At the time of writing a general election is expected in the next couple of years. There is therefore no guarantee that the IRP will come to fruition, and to what extent this will effect operations in Glasgow and in Scotland more widely is uknown.

Glasgow's Canals

With the close proximity of ironstone and coal, the birth of Scotland's iron and steel industry had begun in 1759 at the Carron Iron Works near Falkirk and there then emerged an urgency to move this heavy product to the west. This need produced what was Scotland's largest civil engineering project of the time. When it opened in 1790, the Forth and Clyde Canal was quickly being used to transport over 3 million tons of goods each year. The canal also sparked growth, encouraging the building of factories, breweries, distilleries and foundries. Besides iron coming to the foundries in the west, firebricks came from G. R. Stein's works at Manuel, Whitecross, between Glasgow and

The Forth and Clyde Canal at Cadder, Bishopbriggs. This style of bascule bridge crossed the canals throughout their length and disappeared as the canals closed. (Michael Meighan Collection)

Edinburgh. It was once the largest maker of the fireclay brick in the Empire, and which was to be so important in the manufacture of steel.

The Forth and Clyde Canal Co. was incorporated under a 1768 Act of Parliament and finally opened in 1790 having suffered a hiatus for several years from 1775 due to lack of funds. It was resurrected with the help of government funds, much of it from estates confiscated from the defeated Jacobites after the 1746 Battle of Culloden.

The canal was a highly successful enterprise. Not only did it allow for the transportation of raw materials to factories and docks in the west but it allowed those in the east to trade with Ireland and beyond as well as improve access to Europe and the Baltic for products such as tobacco from Glasgow. A major advantage was the fact that vessels could head for the Atlantic or North Sea via the canal and not go round the south coast. In time of war this was a hazardous journey with ships sometimes having to travel in convoy because of the danger of attack from French ships during the Napoleonic Wars.

From the Firth of Forth, the best alignment of the canal took it north of Glasgow through Bishopbriggs, Maryhill, Anniesland and Clydebank, finally joining the Clyde at Bowling. In order to bring the canal into the city centre as well as connect with the Monkland Canal, a spur was built from Maryhill to Port Dundas in the north of the city. Port Dundas was to quickly become a major industrial area hosting the famous, now closed, White Horse Distillery as well as chemical factories, textile mills and glass and pottery works. It was also the site of the Pinkston Power Station that was built in 1900 to provide electricity for the newly electrified Glasgow Corporation Tramways.

Pinkston Power Station on the Forth and Clyde Canal. (Michael Meighan Collection)

On Speirs Wharf were the offices of the Forth & Clyde Navigation Co. and the City of Glasgow Grain Mills and Stores built for John Currie & Co. in 1851. The buildings were converted in 1989 into 150 loft-style residential apartments, a private leisure centre, and nineteen commercial units.

The 12-mile-long Monklands Canal, started in 1770, was first opened to bring coal from the Lanarkshire coalfields. There was coal under Glasgow but a poor road network surrounding the city and a cartel of mine owners in and around Glasgow was controlling the price of coal to keep it high. The Monkland Canal was a means to bring cheaper coal into the city, and it worked, albeit after overcoming a series of difficulties in construction. These included a bottleneck in locks at Blackhill that was solved by the construction of a ship lift. This was basically a huge tank on rails that carried barges up a slope, bypassing the four sets of lock gates that were causing the bottleneck. The lift was only used when the water supply to the locks was low, but even then 7,500 boats passed through from around 1850 to 1887. The canal started in Calderbank, near Airdrie, and eventually terminated in Townhead, but not until 1794.

As the nineteenth century wore on and as the Lanarkshire steelworks developed, the canal played an evermore important part in transporting steel, iron and finished goods to Glasgow and the Clyde.

With the coming of the railways, both canals became a second transport option and began to lose profit. The Monkland Canal was taken over by the Caledonian Railway

Speirs Wharf. (Michael Meighan Collection)

Company, who didn't have a great deal of interest in making it competitive. In the 1930s it fell into disuse as trains and lorries began to transport heavy goods and was finally closed to navigation in 1950. The route of the canal from Townhead to Easterhouse then provided a ready route for the new Monkland Motorway, part of the new M8, the building of which took many years but considerably improved travel between Edinburgh and Glasgow. There are remaining portions of the canal in Drumpellier Country Park, Coatbridge, and it also forms part of the Summerlee Heritage Park that hosts the wonderful Museum of Industrial Life.

Back when I was a boy, the network of canals in Scotland was all but closed and was fairly smelly too but it was a great joy to me to be able to cycle to Bowling all the way along the Forth and Clyde Canal. I can do that once again for, with a £94 million grant from the Millennium Commission, the Forth and Clyde Canal was reopened in 2001. Bridges and locks have been replaced and once again boats ply their way. The banks now provide fine walking and I have even seen fishing. The

Anglers enjoy some fishing on the canal. (Michael Meighan, with permission)

The *Gipsy Queen*. Excursions from Port Dundas were very popular. (Michael Meighan Collection)

canal is now a major tourist attraction and central to that at the eastern end is the Falkirk Wheel and the Kelpies sculptures, near to where the Carron Ironworks once stood.

It is a magnificent thing that the Forth and Clyde Canal is now reopened all the way to the East Coast. Now you can walk or cycle all the way to Edinburgh, or maybe just from Speirs Wharf at Port Dundas to Maryhill where the restored canal link now meets the Forth and Clyde.

But we haven't finished with canals, for there was another one, a canal that is little known about in Glasgow but certainly is known in Paisley. This was the Glasgow, Paisley and Johnstone Canal. In 1791, the Earl of Eglinton formed a company to build a canal from Glasgow to Ardrossan. Twenty years later, in 1811, the section between the Glasgow terminal at Port Eglinton and Johnstone, at Thorn Brae, was complete but it never reached Ardrossan because the money ran out. Port Eglinton is, of course, remembered in Glasgow's Eglinton Street, adjacent to where the canal began.

The canal opened with the launch of the *Countess of Eglinton* barge, but it was only four days after the launch, on 10 November, that disaster struck when the overloaded *Countess*, packed with passengers taking advantage of the Martinmas Fair holiday, capsized hurling 100 passengers into the water, eighty-five of whom drowned or were crushed in the confusion.

With the rise of the railways, while the canal was initially very busy with both passengers and cargo, it fell into disuse and was purchased by the Glasgow & South Western Railway Company. It closed in 1881 to become the Paisley Canal Line from Ardrossan to Glasgow. The line closed to passengers in 1983 but in 1990 passenger services resumed from Glasgow Central station to a new Paisley Canal station with much of the abandoned track beyond becoming a cycle and walkway.

'Kid on your daft and ye'll get a hurl for nothing' – On the Tram

You would hardly meet any Glaswegian of my vintage who would tell you that getting rid of the trams was a good idea. Thinking back, you wonder why the circle has turned and trams appear to be the transport of the future, in other cities at least? For at one time

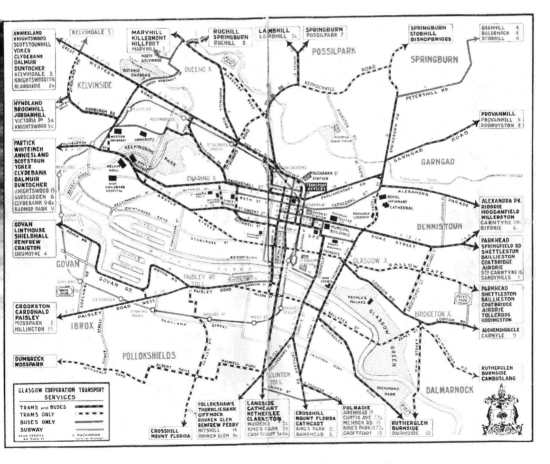

The Glasgow Tram and Subway network in 1935. (Michael Meighan Collection)

in Glasgow, getting rid of trams in favour of the petrol engine was considered to be the future of public transport.

Glasgow Corporation Tramways was to become the largest urban tram system in Europe and was the last of the old systems to close when the last tram ran in 1962. It was with quite a fanfare that Glasgow finally said goodbye to the tramcar. I was standing there at the corner of Argyle Street and Oswald Street watching as the parade went past and there were tears in people's eyes. The trams had only recently seen them through the Second World War and were always there when you needed them even though you might get frustrated with the traffic jams.

It is said that the world's first passenger tram route was the Swansea & Mumbles Railway in South Wales. The line was originally built to transport coal and other minerals, with Parliamentary permission given to transport passengers from March 1807. Steam trams were introduced in 1877, with electrics commencing in 1929. It was finally closed in 1961. This venture was the work of Benjamin French, who offered to run the service and paid the owning company a fee to do so. The tramway was born and so too was the first railway station, at The Mount. We were walking two years ago at The Mumbles and we had no idea that we were on the route of that famous tramway. It is a lovely area.

The idea for trams in Glasgow actually came from two separate London syndicates who proposed bills in Parliament to construct tramlines in the city. Both bills were opposed by Glasgow Corporation but after some negotiation they allowed an amalgamation of the bills but with the clever clause allowing them to take over the enterprise within

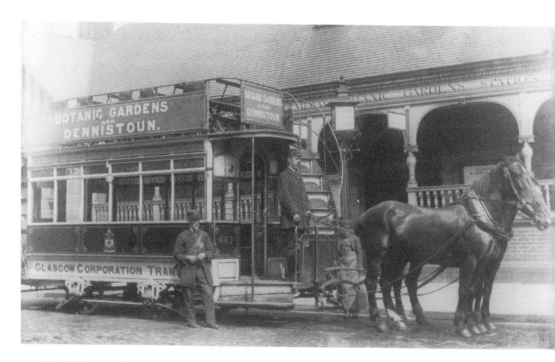

No. 463 car at Botanic Gardens railway station. It is heading along Great Western Road towards Dennistoun. This was to become Service No. 1. (Michael Meighan Collection)

six months of passing of the Act. Within that period the Corporation decided that they would exercise their right and took over ownership of the lines but allowed the original promoters to form a new company and lease the lines for twenty-three years.

By August 1872, the first horse-drawn trams were ready to run and the system was inaugurated with great fanfare on 20 August. *The Glasgow Herald* reported: 'Yesterday forenoon, by invitation of the Glasgow Tramway and Omnibus Company, the Lord Provost, magistrates, town council and a large number of gentlemen assembled at St. George's Cross in order to formally open the line.'

Seven trams had been brought from the Cambridge Street depot and lined up along Great Western Road, some with two horses abreast, some with three. All were supervised by smartly uniformed staff. Just before noon, the lead tram, hosting the Lord Provost and entourage, moved off through a thronging crowd, making its way steadily round the curves of Cambridge Street into Sauchiehall Street. This first run was to the top of Eglinton Street. The record shows that the official gentlemen were a bit disappointed at the slow speed of progress. Maybe someone was showing off as the return trip to the depot in Cambridge Street took only thirteen minutes. Try doing that now at any time of day!

I discovered only recently that one of the original tram depots had been in my street and known by myself and others as 'Greig's Wool Store'. It was a huge brick building

Horse trams and carts in Jamaica Street by George Washington Wilson. (Michael Meighan Collection)

from where I used to collect stamps delivered to them on letters from Pakistan and elsewhere, presumably to where they were sending the large bales of wools stored within the building. Inside, above the bales, the large factory-like centre was ringed with two or three levels of gantries leading to more entrances. It all made sense when I discovered that this was once one of a number of depots with trams housed at ground level and the horses stabled above. Along with the next-door cemetery and virtually all of North Street, that building was to be swept away by the new M8 motorway.

The company ownership of the tram system lasted only twenty years, for it was then taken over by Glasgow Corporation. It decided that they would not renew the leases and would run the trams themselves. By that time, in 1894, the GTOC had become a major private monopoly called familiarly 'The Company'. It now owned 2,000 horses, 233 tramcars and twenty-four omnibuses.

This period in the 1800s was one of considerable unrest. It was the time of the Highland Clearances when crofters and labourers and their families had been forced off their homesteads to make way for sheep and agricultural improvements. While this led to a Royal Commission on crofting tenures in 1883 and legislation in 1886, whole impoverished families by then had moved from country to city with few skills other than their ability to handle horses, a skill much in demand by the growing transport and haulage companies.

However, it was also a time of huge unemployment in Great Britain with companies forcing long hours and low wages on their employees. It was not unknown for carters to

Greig's Wool Store/former tram depot of the Glasgow Tramway and Omnibus Company. (Michael Meighan)

be working from 5.00 a.m. till 8.00 p.m. From these conditions emerged a fightback that was to become known as 'Red Clydeside' and which had its origins in such conflicts in which the horsemen found themselves in the early days of public transport.

In 1886, throughout Great Britain, there had been demonstrations against low wages and in 1889 there was considerable industrial unrest on the west coast of Scotland within passenger transport. Of particular concern were the conditions imposed upon tramway servants by The Company, who were requiring staff to work up to seventeen hours a day for 20s a week – considered a miserable sum at the time. A committee of workers was formed to consider action. Following a meeting to protest, the twenty members of the committee were summarily sacked by the employer. The recently formed trades council passed a resolution of protest in June 1889 and called for municipal ownership.

While it tends to have been passed by in any history of Glasgow, this event had momentous consequences for the transport industry and for passenger transport in and around the city. The campaign for public ownership became central to the Trades Union movement in Scotland and was the basis for a campaign leading to a strike of Scotland-wide carters in August of that year. Although the strike lasted barely a fortnight, it was to have a considerable effect on industrial relations in the future. Some private contractors agreed higher wages, and payment for overtime, which had long been denied.

The day following the strike was the historic London dock strike. This, along with other campaigns, raised the morale of Scottish workers and gave huge impetus to the formation of trades unions. In September of that year came a march by the Glasgow United Trades Council in support of the Tramway Servants and the demand for Glasgow Corporation to take over tramway services from The Company. Such was the strength of feeling in the council that the carters and horsemen representing tram drivers and others were put at the head of the procession, which numbered 13,000 men of many trades.

This campaign was kept up for four years and had a huge impact on public opinion, becoming a local election issue. It was instrumental in bringing the trams under public ownership by the Corporation in 1894. Not surprisingly The Company was a bit miffed and decided that they would not sell their trams to the Corporation, who then had to shell out for their own cars and ancillary equipment.

The Corporation ran their first service on 1 July 1894. Quite incredibly, within a year there were 250 trams on the road. By 1956, there were 1,966 trams and buses on our streets carrying 661,339,964 passenger journeys with an income of £9 million. By the way, The Company continued to run their own competing omnibus service for a while, but eventually conceded defeat.

Meanwhile the network too had expanded to encompass the surrounding towns and villages that could not afford, or did not want to run, their own services. For instance, Airdrie and Coatbridge Tramways was bought by the Corporation in 1921 and the Paisley District Tramways Company in 1923. In this way trams went for long distances, sometimes running on lines through the countryside to towns and villages including Airdrie, Renfrew, Bishopbriggs, Cambuslang and Paisley.

Even as they had started running, technology was moving ahead and as early as 1896 experts thought that horse-drawn trams were out of date. While the first Corporation horse tram started service in 1894, it was only four years later, in October 1898, that the first experimental electric tram made its appearance, making its run from Springburn in the north of the city to Mitchell Street.

Besides the provision of 400 new trams, the decision to electrify and expand meant the building of new infrastructure. An independent electricity supply was needed and this came from a temporary generator while a new coal-fired power station was built on the banks of the Forth and Clyde Canal in Pinkston up in Port Dundas, above the city. A number of sub-stations were also required, as was the complex system of overhead wires to which the pantographs on the trams would be attached. Bear in mind that this might be done by the erection of poles to support the wires. However, if you have a look at the fronts of older Glasgow buildings you might still see the metal hooks (rosettes) to which the supporting wires were attached. At this time Glasgow was undergoing substantial building work, so the attachment of cables and the placing of poles must have been extremely complicated.

The electric trams were much heavier than those previously needed for horse trams. New, heavier rails were needed and in many cases these would have to be bedded into the granite cobbles or 'setts'. The other issue was trains. Glasgow was an industrial city with factories and yards throughout the centre. Provision was made for this by ensuring that the tram gauge was able to accommodate railway traffic that might, on occasion, use the tramlines.

I remember my father telling me about the first electric 'caurs'. Using the term for a common type of flatted apartment in Glasgow, the trams were nicknamed the 'room and

Run for it Hen! 'Vestibule cars' on a very busy corner of Union Street and Argyle Street before Boots the Chemist set up shop. (Michael Meighan Collection)

Work tram laying granite setts on Glasgow's Broomielaw. (Michael Meighan Collection)

kitchen'. Twenty of these single-deck trams entered service in 1898. My dad said they were so named because there was a saloon to either side of a central entrance and women would use one side while men would use the other. I don't know whether this was true but what is true is that one was non-smoking and the end that was for smokers had windows with waterproof blinds but no glass.

The room and kitchens were unsuccessful and only lasted eight years, but car 672 had been kept as a testing vehicle and survived the dismantling of this unusual fleet. You can see it in Glasgow's wonderful Riverside Museum.

I discovered that the Scottish Tramway and Transport Society was founded specifically to save car 672. They continued to work towards preservation and were successful with a number that are in working order in the National Tramway Museum at Crich, near Matlock in Derbyshire. The society publishes a magazine, *Scottish Transport*, as well as other books of interest to tram enthusiasts.

At the beginning of electrification as the demand was so great, 120 modified redundant horse car bodies were fitted onto new trolleys. They mostly lasted only to the beginnings of the First World War, although one was still running in the 1930s. The mainstay of the Glasgow fleet was the four-wheeled double-decker Standard car of which 1,000 were built between 1898 and 1924. Many lasted from electrification well into the 1950s, although there were four phases of modernisation.

We are used to seeing these early trams in black and white but, in fact, it wasn't the case, for they were actually quite colourful. Bear in mind that in those early days, until

Standard cars on Argyle Street, posted 1917. These cars had back and front outside platforms. (Michael Meighan Collection)

the wider impact of education for all, many people were illiterate. Looking at the some of the pictures here you might wonder how they knew which trams were theirs? That was because each tram route had a coloured band on the tram to identify it. For instance, Route 1, the Botanic Gardens to Dennistoun route, had a green band and others, red, blue yellow and green. With their broad coloured banding, their original orange panelling and brown-framed windows, they would have actually made quite a colourful spectacle in the city centre. The coloured banding was phased out between 1937 and 1952, leaving the Glasgow Corporation colours of orange, green and cream.

In 1915 when young men were being sent to the front during the First World War, there was a need to keep the trams running and this, and the fulfillment of other occupations, could only be achieved by the employment of women. During the conflict, battalions were formed from factories, offices and other organisations. The 15th Highland Light Infantry (Tramways Battalion) was formed and 1,000 volunteers were recruited by the General Manager, James Dalrymple. This left a severe shortage of staff and women were then recruited as conductors. Their uniform consisted of a green jacket and long skirt in Corporation of Glasgow green tartan. By 1916 there were 1,180 women conductors and twenty-five drivers. The picture overleaf shows the first Glasgow 'Clippie' giving a ticket to a gentleman. Very smart the pair of them.

To begin with, the new trams had open tops just like the horse trams. Roofs were added, although, to begin with, there were open balconies at either end. The first cars had

Tram conductress in 1915 on a Standard round dash with added glazed panels. (Michael Meighan Collection)

rounded fronts (dash panels) and the cars were then called 'round dash'. Later Standard cars had glazed vestibules and were given hexagonal dash panels and these were known as 'hex dash'. Eventually all Standard cars were upgraded and received glazed vestibules.

On 18 May 1931 a hex dash tramcar went off the rails in Dumbarton Road and careered into the Scotstoun Emporium at Primrose Street. This was a 'Kilmarnock bogie'

No. 26 Standard hex dash in Argyle Street at Finnieston heading to Clydebank. That's a Hillman Minx parked. (Michael Meighan Collection)

and according to some experts they were not good on tight curves and had to be confined to a small number of straighter routes. The Kilmarnock bogie appeared in the late 1920s as part of a modernisation of the trams when serious competition from motor buses began. They were designed by the Kilmarnock Engineering Company but built by English Electric in Preston. Their official name was the Maximum Traction Bogie.

It might interest you to know that the story was picked up by a famous Italian newspaper, *La Domenica del Corriere*, and an image by the well-known Italian artist Achille Beltrame featured on the front page. Why? For many years there have been links between Italy and Scotland and it would not have been unusual for Italian newspapers to carry stories of what was happening here. While we know about fish and chips and ice cream, think about some of the well-known names originating in Italy: Daniela Nardini, Nicola Benedetti, Tom Conti, Richard Demarco, Paolo Nutini and many more.

'A tramcar, suddenly derailed, fell against the window of a large china shop, smashing everything and frightening the passers-by.' (Drawing by A. Beltrame) (Michael Meighan Collection)

A cobbled Argyle Street with a bread van from the famous Beatties Bakery. There's the Argyll Arcade too. A Scammell Scarab waits behind the tram. (Michael Meighan Collection)

In the 1930s, as the Standard car was looking very tired, and some cities were abandoning their tram routes, the Corporation took the bold step of designing two new prototypes. A stimulus to this was the need for new transport for visitors to the Empire Exhibition in Bellahouston Park in 1938. With an eye to the new streamlined age, the new trams had superior interiors and, as they were introduced during the year of the Coronation of King George VI, they became known as Coronation Cars. Between 1948 and 1952, the Coronation Mark II emerged. 100 of these, with more rounded cabs, were built and with an acknowledgement to the launch of the Cunard RMS *Queen Mary* in 1936, they became known as 'Cunarders'.

Glasgow's electric trams had a long and proud history seeing a variety of new and experimental models. Trams first began to be phased out in 1949 and as trolleybuses and diesel buses entered service there were further reductions, with the final trams running in September 1962.

Such was the sentimental attachment to the 'caurs' that, on a wet day, 250,000 people lined a route from Dalmarnock Road to Albert Drive via the city centre to watch a procession of twenty of the city's historic and modern trams. I was one of those laying a penny on the rail to have it flattened as a 'caur' went over it. What memories! While there are presently no tramcars on Glasgow streets, the story may not be quite over, for under a Scottish government review of mass transit, there are plans for new metros throughout the Glasgow area. These will be part of a major thirty-year development that will better

Two Standard trams at Glasgow Cross. (Michael Meighan Collection)

Shawlands Cross. While tram staff are waiting for their new shifts, an inspector is waiting to board a tram or bus to check tickets. (Michael Meighan Collection)

School for training drivers with a skeleton car behind, complete with all wiring and controls. (Michael Meighan Collection)

connect more than 1.5 million people to employment, education, and health services. The Clyde Metro has been confirmed as a key priority for future transport investment and we may then see new heavy and light metros, as well as new stations and connections throughout the greater Glasgow area.

If you visit Glasgow's wonderful Riverside Museum you will see fine examples of Glasgow's old trams. The Museum of Scottish Industrial Life at Summerlee in Coatbridge also has a Glasgow single-decker tram that was originally part of the Paisley fleet.

I'm on the Bus

We can't really tell exactly when bus services started in and around Glasgow but there is no doubt that as the city grew it enveloped surrounding burghs. As industry expanded along the Clyde local entrepreneurs saw the opportunities in moving people in and out of the city.

Among the very first of these was John Scott Russell. Russell built the SS *Great Eastern* steamship with Brunel and designed the famous HMS *Warrior*, now restored and berthed in Portsmouth. Less successfully he introduced the first steam carriage between Glasgow and Paisley.

Unfortunately one of his vehicles was held responsible for the first fatal bus crash. His bus, built in 1834 for the Scottish Steam Carriage Company, carried twenty-six passengers between Glasgow and Paisley. Unfortunately those who objected to the new

Charabancs wait at the south end of the Jamaica Bridge. (Michael Meighan Collection)

transport were accused of sabotaging it by creating a roadblock that overturned the carriage. The boiler blew up killing five passengers. The service was discontinued but two of the carriages were moved to London to operate.

Meanwhile others were using more conservative methods. One of the first of these was Wylie and Lochhead, a company that was to become well known in Glasgow history, particularly in undertaking and cabinetmaking. Around 1837 they were the first to run horse bus services between Partick and Glasgow, using an old-fashioned stagecoach. This was replaced with a custom-built horse omnibus running a service every two or three hours at a flat fare of 4*d* (old pence).

In 1847 James 'Hookey' Walker began two services from Partick to Glasgow, one via Finnieston and Anderston, another from Dowanhill to the Royal Exchange.

Just as there is competition now there was then for, around 1856, a consortium of six business people in Partick started up the Glasgow and Partick Omnibus Company and Wylie and Lochhead discontinued their services.

With the introduction of the petrol engine the old stagecoaches disappeared and for a while were replaced by the charabanc, basically an open coach with bench seats often used for day excursions.

Glasgow Corporation Transport

The growth of bus services in and around Glasgow saw start-ups, mergers and takeovers with Glasgow Corporation becoming one of the first large operators. The Corporation

Halley's Industrial Motors single-decker, one of Glasgow Corporation's first buses. (Michael Meighan Collection)

had succeeded Glasgow Town Council in 1895 and ran buses from 1924. In 1929 Glasgow Corporation Tramways was renamed Glasgow Corporation Transport Department and became responsible for all bus, tram and underground services.

One of the first Glasgow Corporation buses was a single-decker on a Halley chassis, purchased locally, for Halley's Industrial Motors operated from a factory based in Yoker. The coachwork was by Law, based in nearby Scotstoun. Registered in 1906, Halley's took over the business of the Glasgow Motor Lorry Co. Halley's was to become one of the top commercial vehicle manufacturers in Great Britain, contributing hugely to the movement of troops and supplies during the First World War. For some reason, Halley's provided only two of the fourteen buses ordered by the Corporation, others being provided by Tilling, Stevens, Bristol, AEC, Leyland and Thornycroft. Halley's went into liquidation in 1927 but was rescued by the North British Locomotive Co. The firm closed in 1935 and was acquired by Albion Motors.

Following the purchase of the first fourteen buses, the next were Leyland Lions from 1927. No. 18 is seen heading up Clarence Drive towards St Vincent Street. This was the first Leyland chassis specifically designed for a bus body. It may still have been in service in 1949.

From 1928, a fleet of new revolutionary double-deckers, Leyland Titans, were used on the first cross-city route from Knightswood to King's Park, joining up two of Glasgow's new housing estates. Between 1928 and 1931 a total of 258 of the TD1 type entered service. This huge addition to the bus fleet put paid to the small, independent bus operators that had been illegally picking up passengers within the city boundary.

This Glasgow Corporation Leyland Lion GD 7575 is heading up Clarence Drive towards St Vincent Street. (Michael Meighan Collection)

CORPORATION BUS TOURS

The Ideal Way to See Glasgow

BUSES LEAVE GEORGE SQ. DAILY FROM 2 P.M. —JUNE TO SEPTEMBER

ALL BUSES EQUIPPED WITH MICROPHONES AND LOUD SPEAKERS

Sit . Look . Listen

Enquiry Office : 45 COCHRANE ST. (George Square)

In the 1930s, Corporation bus and tram excursions were very popular. (Michael Meighan Collection)

This competition for fares, and for cargos in the case of lorries, was causing mayhem on the roads, which at the time were not suitable for heavy vehicles travelling at speed. As road traffic increased so did accidents and deaths. Throughout the 1920s drivers of public vehicles were pushed to work excessively long hours, becoming a danger to themselves and to other road users and roads were becoming increasingly dangerous to cross. Twelve hours of driving was common, and often exceeded, with drivers prompted to race each other with unreasonably timed stops, resulting in excessive speeds.

The availability of motor vehicles (often ex-military, sold off by the Government Disposals Board, and suitable for adaptation), along with the availability of hire purchase, had encouraged many new small transport businesses, all touting for the travelling public. Ex-servicemen had often invested in these, running them as goods vehicles during the week and, fitted with bench seats, as buses at the weekend. After considerable pressure, particularly from trades unions, and from the larger transport companies, studies were carried out and representations invited from all interested parties. This resulted in the 1930 Road Traffic Act introduced by Herbert Morrison.

The Act produced a wide range of controls, restrictions and responsibilities. The first of these was the driving licence: 'A person shall not drive a motor vehicle on a road unless he is the holder of a licence, and a person shall not employ any person to drive a vehicle unless the person so employed is the holder of a licence, and if any person acts in contravention of this provision, he shall be guilty of an offence.'

As far as public transport was concerned it did a number of things: it introduced a 30 mph speed limit for public service vehicles. Besides classifying public service vehicles (PSVs), it limited the number of hours a driver could be at the wheel and introduced a wide range of rules affecting drivers, conductors and passengers on public vehicles. Most importantly, it gave local authorities the power to run public service vehicles. While Glasgow Corporation had already begun to do so, it was the beginnings of a wider, nationally regulated public service that was to last until bus deregulation in 1986 when services returned to much of the mayhem described above.

With increasing speed Glasgow enlarged its bus fleet while modernising its trams. By 1931 there were 331 buses, but by 1948 there were almost 1,000 buses and trolleybuses carrying 260 million passengers a year. Housing all of these buses necessitated building huge bus garages. The first purpose-built garage was Larkfield, Govanhill, in 1929 followed by Maryhill, Knightswood and Hampden.

After the Second World War, as bus services throughout Great Britain expanded, so did the provision of buses and bus chassis. Glasgow Corporation experimented with many of the manufacturers but initially made extensive use of AEC buses, a front-engined double-decker built from 1945.

The ending of tram services, in September 1962, happened just after I left primary school in Anderston. I was used to taking the tram from Anderston Cross to Glasgow Cross and then up the High Street on a trolleybus as my secondary school was in the same direction as my grannie. In fact, I was very used to trams at Anderston Cross. The Cross was a tram terminus and when I was a wee boy, I was allowed to set the car seats back to face the correct direction and change the points on the rails using the point setter, a metal rod with a sharp handle that you push between the rails at the points to move them.

Restored Glasgow Corporation 1949 Albion Venturer CX37. (Michael Meighan Collection)

Alexander-bodied Leyland Titan 1961 with an Alexander-bodied Daimler behind. (Martin Deutsch)

It was probably a short time during which we were able to take the tram before it was replaced by a double-decker No. 62 bus. That was a very different experience but not as big a change and surprise that awaited me one day when, as I approached the bus stop I saw that it was a very different kind of bus, with, as it seemed to me, a huge front window and where you would board the bus right beside the driver. This was my first experience of the Leyland Atlantean, an innovative vehicle that would revolutionise bus travel as it paved the way for full-scale one-man operation on Glasgow buses. The engine was in the rear, the entrance in the front beside the driver, and the low chassis gave excellent access.

The Atlantean was born out of the need to modernise and economise as passenger numbers fell after the Second World War when car use was increasing rapidly. Leyland led the way with experimental prototypes and launched the first production model in 1958. Thereafter, the Atlantean was an outstanding success with orders in Scotland being placed by Glasgow Corporation, Aberdeen, Edinburgh and the Scottish Bus Group. By 1972, 6,000 Atlanteans were in service and by the end of production 15,000 had been built.

Glasgow was an early adopter, putting their first Atlantean on the road in December of the same year. After Greater Manchester, Glasgow Corporation became the largest operator of Atlanteans, the coachwork all being provided by Walter Alexander in Falkirk.

Leyland Atlantean at Govan Cross with police box, public toilets and the existing Walter Macfarlane cast-iron fountain. (Michael Meighan Collection)

W. Alexander & Sons Ltd

Typical of the early start-ups was Alexander's Motor Services, which began in Camelon, Falkirk, in 1913 with a lorry fitted with bench seats. By 1924, the company had taken the name W. Alexander & Sons Ltd and in 1929 it was taken over by the Scottish Motor Traction Company (SMT). Continuing under the Alexander name, it expanded, taking over the Scottish General Omnibus Group. In 1948, SMT was nationalised, being taken over by the British Transport Commission.

In 1961 Alexander's was split into smaller units in Fife, Midland, and Northern. The Alexander name was discontinued, although their Bluebird logo was used on the successor companies. In 1978 in a rebranding exercise the three companies became

Alexander's Bluebirds. No better way to see the glories of Scotland. (Michael Meighan Collection)

Alexander's busmen take a break in front of their Leyland Tiger. (James Meighan Collection)

Fife Scottish, Kelvin Scottish and Midland Scottish, Strathtay Scottish and Northern Scottish. They had also been building bodies since 1924 for themselves and for other bus operators. At the time of the Labour government's Transport Act of 1947, the coachbuilding side was separated to continue in the private sector. It continued to do this, although now under the name Alexander Dennis. It is still based in Falkirk and, although it is now under Canadian ownership, it is the UK's largest bus and coach manufacturer.

Scottish Motor Traction

The AEC Regent shown was operated by Western Scottish Motor Traction (SMT). Scottish Motor Traction (SMT) was founded in Edinburgh in 1905 by William Johnston Thompson and operated buses throughout central Scotland. Legislation allowing railway companies to invest in buses allowed the London & North Eastern Railway Company (LNER) and the London, Midland & Scottish Railway to take major stakes in SMT in 1929. They also acquired control of Walter Alexander & Sons bus services as well as their coachbuilding operations.

This SMT AEC Regent may be a football special. (Michael Meighan Collection)

With the growth of SMT, their operations were decentralised; Central SMT operated in Lanarkshire with red buses, Western SMT in south-west Scotland also with red buses and green buses for their east of Scotland routes.

When bus companies were nationalised in 1948 by the Atlee government, SMT was transferred to the new British Transport Commission subsidiary Scottish Omnibuses. SMT sales, service and insurance continued in private hands. Highland Omnibuses was added in 1952.

In 1961 a holding company, Scottish Omnibuses Group (Holdings), was formed. It was renamed the Scottish Bus Group in 1963 and it became part of the new Scottish Transport Group in 1969 when David MacBrayne ferry services were also added. At that time it operated around 4,700 buses and coaches. This comprised Central SMT, W. Alexander & Sons, Scottish Omnibuses, Highland Omnibuses, Western SMT and David MacBrayne.

In 1985, as bus deregulation approached, SBG was restructured into thirteen operating companies. The Scottish Bus Group was dissolved in 2006.

Western SMT Leyland Leopard with an Alexander body leaves Anderston bus station. (Michael Meighan Collection)

McGills Bus Services

McGills is Scotland's largest independent bus company and a great survivor in the history of Scottish buses. McGills Bus Services started in Barrhead in 1933 and expanded considerably up to bus deregulation when it sold out to Clydeside 2000. They kept the McGills name to begin with but then changed to Arriva Scotland West and it was joined by another local company, Ashton Coaches (GMS).

When Arriva decided to abandon the loss-making enterprise in Inverclyde, it was bought by a former GMS owner and the Easdale family with the McGill name being resurrected. The fleet presently consists of around 440 buses and they can be seen regularly in Buchanan bus station. The picture shows a McGills Leyland National of 1987 on the Barrhead run. The Leyland National was a joint project between the National Bus Company and British Leyland between 1972 and 1985. Design was Italian by the sports car designer Giovanni Michelotti, who had previously designed for Triumph and Scammell and others. Over 7,000 Nationals were built until eventually replaced by the Leyland Lynx.

You will still see Nationals around as many were refurbished for deregulation. You might be confused if you had seen a National on the railways as a derivative railbus was produced in a very similar style and with common components.

McGills Leyland National 1987. (Michael Meighan Collection)

All Change on the Buses

Earlier, we saw how the Road Traffic Act of 1930 had introduced regulations for the operation of bus services, allowing local authorities to run them. This did not disallow private companies from running services but ensured that they followed the same regulations and were monitored by Traffic Commissioners, who oversaw operations throughout Great Britain.

However, by the 1960s, it was clear that there was little co-ordination between different operators, public and private. A long sought-after integrated traffic policy simply wasn't there. In order to make public transport more efficient and responsive to passenger needs, Passenger Transport Executives (PTEs) were set up in several major conurbations under the Transport Act of 1968. One of these was the Greater Glasgow Passenger Transport Executive (GGPTE), formed on 1 June 1973. It took over the running of trains and buses throughout the Clyde Valley.

With local government reorganisation in 1975, Strathclyde Regional Council took over and in the 1980s, the Strathclyde Passenger Transport Executive (SPTE) was set up under the control of the regional council.

In 1986, Strathclyde's Buses, a new operating company, while still under the control of Strathclyde Regional Council, inherited the fleet of 800 vehicles from the SPTE, introducing a new black and orange livery for most buses. The company was privatised in February 1993 with a management buy-out taking control. The company was bought for £110 million in May 1996 by FirstGroup. Strathclyde Buses then became First Glasgow.

Strathclyde's Buses VW LT35. (Michael Meighan Collection)

Glasgow belongs to you.

Step on a bus and take the kids to the Transport Museum or Pollok House, the Botanic Gardens, or the model ships at the Art Galleries. Or take a very different look at life and visit the Barrows. While you are about it, don't forget a trip on the Glasgow Underground. It's 80 years old, and the wooden Victorian carriages are oldest in daily use in the world.

Transport Museum:
Buses 21 23 38 38a 39 45 57 59

Pollok House:
Buses 21 23 39 45 57

Botanic Gardens:
Buses 1 2 20 43 58

or Underground to Hillhead

Art Galleries:
Buses 1 6 9 15 16 43 44 56 63 64
or Underground to Partick Cross

 GREATER GLASGOW PASSENGER TRANSPORT EXECUTIVE
48 ST. VINCENT STREET, GLASGOW, G2 5TR Tel: 041-248 5971

An advert for the Greater Glasgow Passenger Transport Executive. (Michael Meighan Collection)

Bus Deregulation

Buses were first regulated under the Road Traffic Act of 1930 and remained virtually unchanged until 1980. While the system of regulation, local council control and licensing may not have changed, the customer changed. With growing use of the car, public transport use halved from the 1950s to the 1980s with unprofitable routes being subsidised by councils.

On 26 October 1986 Margaret Thatcher's Conservative government planned the deregulation of bus and coach services on the basis that privatised services would be more cost-effective and reduce fares. In 1988 the Secretary of State for Scotland, Malcolm Rifkind, announced privatisation in Scotland. In preparation for this the Scottish Bus Group (SBG) was restructured into ten independent bus companies. The sales were completed in 1991, giving £90 million to the government.

With the coming of privatisation, councils had no effective control over who would run buses and new companies could enter the market with only forty-two days' notice. Councils and travel authorities were given the rights to provide services where there was a community need and to provide concessionary fare systems.

The sale ushered in a period of severe and often bitter competition when rival companies vied for passengers. I remember Union Street choked with buses of rival companies trying to stop at the same stops. To add to this was the effect on the environment and health, for redundant, inefficient and polluting buses were brought back into service. It was strange to see old London Routemasters in Glasgow, albeit in the livery of the new companies.

In Scotland, we seem to have come full circle, for, from July 2022, local authorities were able to run their own services. This was a consequence of the Transport (Scotland) Act 2019. While some councils may run their own buses, others may opt to franchise services or work in partnership with operators. There is no doubt that much of this may have been influenced by the success of Lothian Buses, a publicly owned service that is the largest municipal bus service in the UK. It has earned the respect of the travelling public in Edinburgh and has even taken over loss-making private operators on other parts of the east coast.

It has been energetic in introducing state-of-the-art environmentally friendly buses and has recently introduced four fully electric Alexander Dennis double-deckers.

While it may not be Glasgow, those who travel on Edinburgh's buses will know how it could be a model for all Scottish bus services. In the meantime, Aberdeen has Great Britain's first fleet of hydrogen cell-fueled buses and as this technology develops we may well see these on Glasgow's streets.

The Bus Run

Of course, if there were buses then there was the bus run, a particular favourite of the Glaswegian. Whether it was Scouts, Cubs, church, school, club or pub, the yearly bus run was essential for fun and for getting us well out of the smoke and smell of the city. I think my first school bus run was to Ayr, where we were left very much on our own after we were counted off the coach right beside the beach. That's when we were issued with a wee brown paper bag containing a cold Scotch pie, a hard-boiled egg, and probably a sandwich and a bag of crisps. It would be well consumed while we planned out our forays into town or to the beach.

It was almost essential that there would be disasters. There would always be a stupid (alleged) shoplifter. Someone would fall into the boating pond and inevitably one or two would disappear and teachers would fume as one of their body would be sent to track them down while we were counted several times in the vain hope that wee MacDonald was hiding under the seat.

Buses used to set out daily from various points including Killermont Street and Waterloo Street bus stations to various places on the Clyde and to the Trossachs. There were bus runs to suit any occasion, such as the company bus run pictured, which I think was to celebrate my father getting married. There was the pub bus run, which I was never on, but I do remember that The Gaiety Bar had a celebrated bus run that my father would look forward to and I believe that he may even have had a hand in organising.

By the way, the bus companies also used to run popular 'mystery tours' which would take you on an excursion somewhere on the coast or up to the Trossachs. It was good fun and I once had the stupidity to think that this was a good trip on which to invite a girl on an early date. She never turned up and that was a real mystery! We used to call it 'a dizzy'.

My da's bus run. That's my father in the middle with the cigarette. It might be a works gathering celebrating my father's marriage. (Michael Meighan Collection)

Getting out of Glasgow

I was once a poor student and the only way to get to London to make my fortune was on the long-distance bus, an arduous, sleepless overnight experience in the early days of the motorways. I did it once. Never again.

Finally, if you have wondered what happens to old buses, well some became site crew buses, motorhomes or breakdown trucks. Here is one on Maryhill Road having become a chip van. Apparently it also used to service Possilpark.

New Express Service

BETWEEN

EDINBURGH and GLASGOW

Leaving St Andrew Square, Edinburgh and Buchanan St. Bus Station, Glasgow

via New Road

Stopping ONLY at Corstorphine Zoo and Baillieston Traffic Lights

COMMENCING SATURDAY, 24TH NOVEMBER

SCOTTISH   OMNIBUSES   LIMITED

Glasgow to Edinburgh bus. (Michael Meighan Collection)

Not happy about leaving Glasgow? He looks like an important wee man getting on the Glasgow to London coach. (Michael Meighan Collection)

Andy's Fish and Chicken Bar, Maryhill Road. Apparently this ex-bus, an Austin K Series, went round Milton in the mid-1960s when a fish supper was 1/9 (one shilling, nine pence). (Michael Meighan Collection)

'Silent Death' – Glasgow's Trolleybuses

While Glasgow's trolleybuses operated until 1967, Commercial Motor reported in June 1965 that the buses were doomed. The journal stated that 115 buses were in service but were likely to be replaced by motor buses over the following two years. They were losing money compared to the operating profit from the fleet of 1,400 motor buses.

Glasgow Corporation BUT Metro-Cammel trolleybus 106 waits at the terminus. (Michael Meighan Collection)

The history of Glasgow's trolleybuses goes back to 1936 when the Glasgow Transport Committee reported unfavourably following a visit to English cities saying that trolleybuses were not suitable for Glasgow's streets and traffic. However, in 1938 the council approved a deputation to visit Manchester and London to report on their trolleybus systems and to advise on operating a similar system in Glasgow. On 7 September 1938 the council's Transport Finance and Works Committee agreed that an experiment with trolleybuses should be allowed.

However, it was not until after the end of the Second World War that any action was taken on the proposition, with the first services, the 101 between Shawfield and Cathedral Street and the 102 between Polmadie and Riddrie, starting in 1949. There were eventually eight services and the fleet peaked at just under 200, which included ten single-decker versions.

I was privileged, as a small boy, to travel on Glasgow's first trolleybus route, the 102. The route of the 102 was via Aitkenhead Road, Albert Bridge at Glasgow Green, Saltmarket, Glasgow Cross and High Street where I joined it on its route up Castle Street to my granny in Royston Road. It then proceeded without me along Provanmill Road to Riddrie. I loved the trolleybus. It was new, quiet and sleek and reeked modernism.

Glasgow's first thirty-four six-wheeled buses were produced by British United Traction (BUT), a company formed when AEC and Leyland combined their trolleybus manufacture that had been suspended during the Second World War. Bodywork was by Metro Cammell of Birmingham with the exterior decked out in the corporation's livery of orange, green and cream. They could carry seventy passengers: fifty on the lower deck, with ten standing, and thirty above. Inside they were finished to a high quality with seats of green moquette trimmed in leather. Further buses were purchased from BUT, Daimler, Crossley and Sunbeam.

There was some enthusiasm for the trolleybuses with 20,000 passengers turning out to travel on their first day. The strongest supporter, Lord Provost Victor Warren, pointed out in January 1950 that it would be in the interests of national economy and security to expand the use of the Pinkston generators to power trolleybuses which would then replace trams.

There was further pressure to expand the service in 1951 when the Transport Committee urged speed in ordering trolleybuses as they might become unobtainable due to the rearmament programme. The fact that at the time around 85 per cent of the tram fleet was over thirty-five years old was compounding the problem.

The situation was becoming worse in 1954 when the Corporation had rejected General Manager ERL Fitzpayne's recommendation to extend trolleybus services to Rutherglen and to equip Victoria Road for trolleybuses. At that time he reported that there was a shortage of 450 trams and some routes should be converted to motor bus operation. In April 1954 of that year, Commercial Motor reported that Fitzpayne had recommended to the Transport Committee that tenders for 100 motor bus chassis be invited. He reported that the Corporation could not overcome the problems caused by trolleybuses becoming detached from their overhead wires. This was a common problem and kept in a holder under each bus was a long bamboo pole used to reattach the pantograph poles.

Hampden Garage was built to house trolleybuses. Here is a pair of No. 105s with Hampden stadium in the background. (Michael Meighan Collection)

There were also traffic jams caused by broken-down buses – some of which caught on fire from overheating electric motors – and from the diversions and stoppages due to the city's extensive redevelopment plans. While the trolleybus has many advantages, the high cost of maintenance and lack of flexibility were making them uneconomic.

It was June 1955 before tenders were invited for new buses – 135 trolleybuses and 150 diesel buses. The order for trolleybuses was later reduced to 99 Crossley double-deckers and ten BUT single-deckers with Burlingham bodies. These extra-length buses operated on the South Side, away from the city centre.

By June 1966 the days of the trolleybus were numbered. The size of the fleet had been reduced to 120 and at that time services 101 and 102 were withdrawn with buses taking over much of these routes, many of them by the 150 new Leyland Atlanteans ordered in 1965. Realistically, while the idea of the trolleybus was being pushed by some, there did not seem to be a huge appetite in the face of the flexibility and availability of the diesel bus. The experiment had lasted only eighteen years, with the last service ending in 1967. While the safety record was quite good, the quiet-running buses had achieved the notorious title of the 'Silent Death'.

There are only two Glasgow trolleybuses still in existence: a BUT/Burlingham, TBS 13, is displayed at the Riverside Museum and TB78, No. 106 to Mount Florida, at the British Trolleybus Society Museum in Sandtoft.

Single-decker BUT trolleybus in Govanhill, Scotland's last trolleybus advertising Pink Stamps. (Michael Meighan Collection)

Glasgow's Subway –
The Clockwork Orange

The Glasgow District Subway is the third oldest underground in the world after London and Budapest. It was opened in 1896 and until 1901 the flat fare was 1*d* – that is, one old penny. Some people might not know that before decimalisation of the UK's currency in 1971, your cash was in £sd – 'libra solidus denarius', the Latin terms for pound, shilling and pence. Officially it was named the Glasgow Underground from 1936 until 2003 when it reverted to its familiar title, simply the Subway.

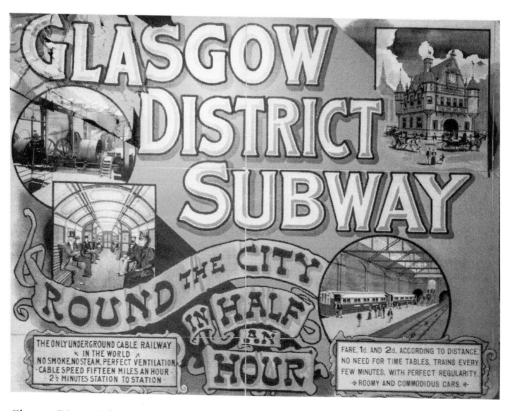

Glasgow District Subway. 'Round the city in half an hour'. (Michael Meighan Collection)

Partick Cross Subway station. Now called Kelvinhall, the entrance is to the east along Dumbarton Road. (Michael Meighan Collection)

When it first opened, single-carriage trains were used. The opening was marred by an accident on the first day when a single carriage carrying sixty passengers was run into by another under the River Clyde. Luckily, there were only four injuries but it caused the Subway to be closed for the first month.

The Glasgow Subway Company was given permission to build the railway using two parallel tunnels under the city. On the 6.5-mile track there are fifteen stations with seven on the South Side and eight in the north.

In 1923, Glasgow Corporation was already running Britain's largest tram network and they took over the running of the Subway at a cost of £385,000. In 1973 the Greater Glasgow Passenger Transport Executive (GGPTE) took over the railway along with most other local rail and bus services in the Clyde Valley.

It is very difficult to describe the smell of the Subway. It smells of damp, from river and other waters seeping in from above. It also has the lingering smell of grease impregnated into the walls and trackbed from the cable that used to run along a channel. The interiors were not unlike our old trams with the pervading smell of leather, polished wood and the sharp odour from the old electric motors and contacts. You might get some sense of the smell when you look at the 1970s photo of Cowcaddens station. The stations were dark and scruffy and you can see the paint falling off due to water seepage and age.

I used to travel on the Subway from a very young age, for fun as a wee boy, and then more regularly as a teenager and adult. I can confirm that the stations and trains were ageing badly and were certainly used less than they had been when both sides of the river would be lined with shipyards and factories. Whole areas of tenements had disappeared and the stations didn't seem to be serving any populations.

When cracks in the tunnels at Govan were discovered, it was decided to close the system down earlier than planned for a complete refurbishment. This entailed the installation of

Cowcaddens station around 1970. (Michael Meighan Collection)

escalators and new platforms and the closure of Merkland Street station and the opening of a new station at Partick to provide a link to the North Clyde Line above. Fittings from the old Merkland Street station form part of the Subway display at the Riverside Museum, which also features three preserved cars.

The Subway is a circular system with trains running on 4-foot tracks in either direction in separate parallel tunnels of either the Inner Circle or Outer Circle. It burrows twice under the River Clyde and the complete journey, if you wanted to take it, would only take around thirty minutes at quiet times.

The rolling stock was first built in 1896 and pulled by a continuous moving cable powered by a steam engine in Scotland Street on the south side of the Clyde. It was converted to electric traction in 1935 and powered by a third rail, running along the side of the tunnel wall. The quality and longevity of the original stock is shown by the fact that the carriages, originally built by the Oldbury Railway Carriage and Wagon Company, and then Hurst Nelson and Company of Motherwell, were only withdrawn from service in 1977 when the system was modernised. One of the features of earlier improvements was the replacement of the old lattice hand-opened gates (like old lifts) with air-operated sliding doors.

The trains were originally painted in cream and plum but became red and white in 1935 then completely red in the 1950s. After the famous Stanley Kubrik 1971 film *A Clockwork Orange* was released in 1971, some people began to call the Glasgow Subway by the same name, possibly because of the new coloured orange trains. Possibly it was because visitors thought the diminutive carriages were more like toy trains.

A refurbished Kelvinhall station. (Michael Meighan Collection)

The new rolling stock built by Metro-Cammell was introduced when the system reopened in 1980. They have continued in use but were refurbished in 1995. Stations were restored and enlarged and became much brighter and fresher.

Many of the stations lie below buildings, so enlarging the tunnels at stations was often out of the question and the limited space meant that some single central platforms have remained. These could be quite dangerous at busy times as the only separation were white lines and a large 'Q' on the platform showing where you should queue for either line. Where it was possible to construct platforms for both lines, one platform has been separated from the track by glass and steel barriers.

While most of Glasgow's Subway stations are more practical than aesthetic, in the centre of St Enoch's Square you will see one of Glasgow's iconic buildings, what was once the entrance to the Subway system. Designed by railway architect James Miller in 1896, it was the ticket office for the railway as well as the headquarters of the Glasgow District Subway Co. The ticket office is no longer an entrance, having been superseded by two canopied stairways. Instead you can enjoy a coffee in the building as it has been converted to a café. And while you are there you might ponder that during the station renovations it was jacked up several feet to allow for building works underneath. The other thing that you might ponder as you sip your coffee and look at the bustling St Enoch Shopping Centre is that where the centre is now was one of Scotland's largest and most elegant

Glasgow Corporation Subway station in St Enoch Square with the demolished St Enoch's Church in the background. (Michael Meighan Collection)

hotels, the St Enoch Hotel. You might also consider how easily you might have travelled to other parts of the city such as Springburn if early plans for extending the Subway had come to fruition, for there were no fewer than six plans, the earliest in 1937, which advocated a line travelling from King's Park, through St Enoch and Buchanan Street, then heading north through Springburn to Robroyston. Five more plans from 1944 to 2010 suggested varying routes, the latest showing a circular route east of the existing circle with extensions to Cathcart and Maryhill, the latter using the unused tunnels that pass under Kelvingrove Park and the Botanic Gardens.

While these plans have all been admirable, the fact is that they would all probably have to be built to modern standards and gauges rather than simply be grafted onto the existing system. The cost of that has always been prohibitive and, as in 1937, wars and other priorities have always got in the way.

In the meantime, the Subway has been showing its age and the existing system is once again being modernised. In 2016, the Strathclyde Partnership for Transport (SPT), successor to the GGPTE, announced a £200 million contract with manufacturers Stadler and Ansaldo STS for modernisation, to include new rolling stock. The new trains were shown to the public at the Berlin InnoTrans 2018 Exhibition. There are seventeen new trains of four, rather than three, carriages as at present, although the overall length will be the same as it is now. They have wider gangways, platform screen doors and will possibly allow driverless operation. The new trains began to be introduced without fanfare in December 2023.

Stadler and Ansaldo STS rolling stock for Glasgow were shown to the public at the Berlin InnoTrans 2018 Exhibition. (FelixM2, Flickr)

Glasgow Subway in Covid days. (Michael Meighan)

The Story of Road Haulage – From Horse and Cart to Diesel Lorries

As I grew up in Anderston, one of my fondest memories of my father was him pontificating on the best ways to get around Scotland and beyond. Before becoming a science teacher he had had careers in the army, where he learned motor mechanics, then as a lorry driver and as a foreman motor mechanic with John McIntosh & Son, a large removal and storage company in Glasgow. His work had taken him throughout the country and he was annoyingly knowledgeable about the best roads to take anywhere, because he had been on them.

While McIntosh and others had been moving over to motor lorries, some were still using the horse, notably Buchanan's Black and White whisky drays, the term usually

Broomielaw Bridge (Jamaica or Glasgow Bridge) by George Washington Wilson. (Michael Meighan Collection)

Argyle Street. No wonder they introduced traffic lights. It must be between 1872 and 1894, for horse trams lasted only around twenty years. (Michael Meighan Collection)

given to local delivery vehicles. Their licensed whisky 'bond' was in Washington Street, leading south from Anderston Cross. From here, the carts, with their distinctive black and white checked patterns, carried loads of horizontally loaded whisky casks or crates to the pubs, bottling plants, docks or railway goods yards.

As business and manufacturing in Glasgow grew, so did the amount of horses and carts (or lurries as they were then called). Here began the seeds of unrest mentioned before with horse trams. As industry grew, the need to move materials grew and this need created a huge haulage industry. Not only were there local independent carters but there were fleets of private hauliers and the railway companies employed many carters, as did the tram company.

The demand for carters was huge but the wages were low, and they were expected to work long hours – from 5.30 a.m. up to fourteen hours a day in some cases. Given the traffic jams in the city centre and around the docks, they might spend long unpaid hours simply waiting to load or unload.

In addition, they were under pressure to carry out a specified number of rakes (journeys) per day, a day being indeterminate, and often they were also expected to manage two wagons at a time, both demanding and hazardous. They worked six days a week, did not finish their day until all was delivered and the horses were returned to the stables and groomed. They were also expected to attend the stables on

Thomas Dickie, dairyman, East John Street and sometime at No. 14 Mordaunt Street and No. 518 Baltic Street in Glasgow's Calton. (Michael Meighan Collection)

a Sunday to groom their horses, again unpaid. It was this behaviour that persuaded Glasgow Corporation to take the running of the horse trams away from a private company in 1894.

Those working for the private haulage companies were not so lucky, but change was on its way with the formation of committees to fight in the first instance for overtime payment and a reduction in the number of rakes. Most of what was asked for was refused by employers. The response from workers was the formation of the Scottish Carter's Association in 1898, which changed its name to the Scottish Commercial Motormen's Union in 1908, finally merging with the Transport and General Worker's Union in 1971. During its time it took part in many of the early industrial disputes including the Forty Hours Strike of 1919, which precipitated the Battle of George Square in which armed forces confronted striking workers, estimated at 20,000–25,000. The union was also instrumental under its various names in promoting the many changes and improvements to the life of the carter and lorry driver. It also heavily influenced legislation for the protection of the road user and pedestrian which resulted in the far-reaching Transport Act of 1930 discussed earlier.

McMartin, the original 'white van man' – possibly groceries or butchery. The wall in the Calton is still there. (Michael Meighan Collection)

The Clydesdale Horse

In researching the story of the carter, it seems to me that the story of the horse has been sadly neglected given the huge numbers that were needed to pull the lurries, not to mention the large number of stables required to house them, as well as the feed that had to be brought in.

From 1837 there existed a system in which stallions were hired throughout Scotland. Local agricultural improvement societies held shows in which the best animals, including stallions, were judged and the owners awarded cash prizes. The heavy horse, particularly the Clydesdale and the Shire Horse, was to change the transport business. The Shire, originally called the Great Horse, is Britain's largest draught horse. Its origins lie in medieval times when it first carried knights into battle, but a breed society was not formed until 1876.

The Clydesdale, first mentioned in 1826, is said to have been bred from imported Flemish horses, a black stallion imported from England by a John Paterson and one owned by the Duke of Hamilton. The horse was named after Clydesdale, an old name for Lanarkshire where the seat of the Duke of Hamilton was at Hamilton Palace and where horse breeding was once a major industry. The Clydesdale horse was to emerge as a recognisable breed by 1840 and by 1945, 20,183 Clydesdale horses had been exported around the world.

As industry in Scotland developed the products of that industry became larger and heavier. Locomotives had to be pulled through Glasgow's streets and canal barges had to be moved long distances at speed. The demands for increasing loads meant stronger horses were needed. The alternative was to pull loads with teams of horses, and ten or more could be seen pulling locomotives and marine engines. In the long term this was unacceptable in busy city streets and to some extent the Clydesdale answered the call until the steam engine appeared.

Left: A horse-driven
road cleaner in
Buchanan Street.
(Michael Meighan
Collection)

Below: Corporation
Water 'Butt' in
Springburn Road
around 1900. (Michael
Meighan Collection)

From Horse and Cart to Lorry

As the industrial age progressed, steam engines were put into use in many areas. The first was the traction engine, a generally cumbersome coal-eating beast that replaced horsepower and pulled a trailer. While there are photographs of them pulling locomotives from the works of the North British Railway Company, they were seldom seen on the main road. Besides pulling circus wagons they also had an attached powered wheel that was used to power equipment such as the generator in the photo, or harvesting machines on farms.

It was just a matter of time before there were successful trials of self-propelled wagons, or lorries, which incorporated the steam engine. One of the most triumphant of these was Glasgow company Alley and McLellan's Sentinel Steam Wagon launched in 1906. The example in the photo might not look much like a lorry as we know them, but these developed over a period of time to include cabs and van bodies.

The internal combustion engine was developing fast in the early part of the twentieth century and while the steam engine competed for a time, the development of heavier petrol lorries put them out of business. By the start of the 1930s some manufacturers had ceased production, gone out of business or moved on to the internal combustion engine. Alley and McLellan, having moved to Shrewsbury in 1915, ceased production in 1938, about the last to do so.

Codona's circus steam engine powering a generator on the wagon. (Michael Meighan Collection)

Scottish Cooperative Wholesale Society Sentinel Steam Wagon. Lofty Peak flour was milled at the Regent Mill on the River Kelvin at Partick. (Michael Meighan Collection)

One of those companies whose origins were in steam engines was the Lancashire Steam Motor Company, which was set up in 1896 by James Sumner and Henry Spurrier. The success of their steam van led them to move to petrol lorries. Their first, nicknamed 'The Pig', was produced from 1904. The name Leyland Motors was adopted in 1907.

One stimulant for the move away from horse and cart to the lorry was the huge number of vehicles that became available following the First World War. One of the

Leyland 'Pig' of John Agnew's Maryhill Cooperage in Ruchill Street, one of many cooperages in the city. (Michael Meighan Collection)

'peace dividends' was the return of thousands of army vehicles. It wasn't a happy time for lorry manufacturers but it was certainly helpful to the haulage industry. To protect its name and reputation Leyland bought 3,000 of these vehicles returning from the front to refurbish and resell. This prevented many of their lorries ending up broken down in the streets.

It was no wonder that I had a fascination with road transport, as I was surrounded by it. In Bishop Street, where I went to primary school, there was a 'carriers quarters'. I can't remember who owned it but it was the base for a haulage company whose lorries would be parked along the street. In the same street was also a Pickfords depot. Pickfords styled themselves as 'The Gentle Giant'. Just round the corner in Douglas Street was another well-known remover, Dawsons, which used articulated pantechnicons.

My father explained to me that following the Second World War, the road transport industry in which he was involved had undergone major changes. In 1948, as a result of the 1947 Transport Act, the haulage industry was nationalised. It comprised British Road Services (BRS), BRS Parcels, Pickfords, Containerway and Roadferry. Most of the larger companies had been absorbed into these, although a few of them, like Pickfords, kept their brand names.

One of those nationalised was the Clyde & Campbeltown Shipping Company that operated from Clyde Street in Glasgow. There is a Hansard record showing that the

Wishaw-registered Ford van of the Clydesdale Chocolate Company. (Michael Meighan Collection)

company stopped running their Glasgow to Lochranza and Campbeltown passenger services in 1939 but continued to provide cargo services. In 1949 the lorries were taken over by British Road Services.

Nationalisation also included railways, sea shipping, ports and the idea was to provide an integrated and planned publicly owned system. The plan was bitterly opposed in parliament and the 1951 Conservative government denationalised transport, but left railways nationalised until John Major's government privatised them between 1994 and 1997.

As industry, local government and the armed services moved from horse and carriage, the opportunities for providing motorised transport seemed endless. These early companies seized these opportunities and thrived at the beginning of the twentieth century mostly due to their ability to turn their skills to the war effort through the mass manufacturing of lorries. This was a time in which the lorry and car were very simple and copying was easy as long as a reliable engine was available. However, the end of the First World War brought a tough time for car manufacture due to a drop in orders, the recession and competition from European manufacturers.

I have particular memories of the Anderston district of Glasgow in the 1950s and 1960s as that was where I lived. One of these memories involves the regular passing of grey-painted vehicles without their coachwork, only the chassis. Even the driver was unprotected as these skeletal vehicles headed eastwards along Argyle Street towards the city. My father explained to me that these chassis had come from the Albion works at

AEC Monarch of the Clyde & Campbeltown Shipping Company built between 1931 and 1939. (Michael Meighan Collection)

Union Street. Horses and carts are now sharing the roadway with lorries. If you look on the left the carter may be having difficulty controlling the horse. The folks on the right are waiting for a tram. I haven't seen the elaborate fare stage sign before. (Michael Meighan Collection)

The Albion delivery van was owned by another iconic Glasgow brand, Creamola, whose custard was famous – 'Tickling the World's Palate'. (Michael Meighan Collection)

Scotstoun. He would have been very familiar with these lorries as he was then a foreman motor mechanic with John McIntosh & Sons in Argyle Street. Albion Motors, 'Sure as the Sunrise', is the best-known name in car and lorry manufacture in Scotland and is to Scotstoun what John Brown's is to Clydebank, just up the road. However, the days of manufacture of lorries and cars have long passed with the last lorry rolling off the production line in the 1970s.

Albion was a successful brand, building up a solid following and a good reputation for quality. It was probably this that attracted a successful takeover bid in 1951 from acquisitive Leyland Motors that had a similar vehicle portfolio. At that time the main products were the Albion Chieftain, Reiver, Clydesdale trucks and the Viking bus.

But back to my father and my mother, because I started this by telling you that it was a very personal story. I found out very early that, not only had my father worked as a motor mechanic, he also drove furniture vans to London and on one occasion while travelling at night without headlights he drove his lorry into a large bomb crater. He survived but would have got quite a fright. So would others, as his large van was full of coffins going from a Glasgow company to Dunkirk – a sobering thought.

My mother, as a firewoman during the Second World War, drove fire equipment to London to help deal with blazes during the Blitz. Both rarely talked of the difficulties in driving large vehicles on the pre-motorway 'A' roads of those times. Driving was heavy, and with no assisted steering it was tiring work, and would take two days to get to London, particularly as signposts had been removed so as not to be helpful to the enemy if they invaded. My mother told me that she would be welcome to rest at fire stations along the way.

A 1950s Austin BMC flatbed owned by R. M. Easdale, scrap merchants, which still exists. (Michael Meighan Collection)

While there was a huge demand for lorries during the war, after it, in Glasgow, there was an increasing demand for vans and lorries as the country began to return to some kind of normality. With the coming of the Bruce Comprehensive Development Area plans, that demand increased as furniture vans began to remove the vast numbers of tenement dwellers out from the city centre to the new schemes and to the new towns of East Kilbride, Cumbernauld and Irvine. A great deal of head scratching ensued when it was discovered that old massive wardrobes, chests, pianos and three-piece suites would not fit into the new houses. Getting them onto the lifts in the high flats was a challenge.

Right: A Morris FE. This is a pantechnicon usually used to move furniture, seen here at St Enoch Square advertising new town living. Probably on hire from Dawsons Removals in Douglas Street. (Michael Meighan Collection)

Below: A Daimler ambulance of the St Andrew's and Red Cross Scottish Ambulance Service. St Andrew's still operates as a first-aid charity. (Michael Meighan Collection)

From Petrol to Diesel

While the diesel engine was invented in Germany in 1897 it did not appear in lorries until Benz introduced it in 1923. It was not common in the UK until reliable manufacturers appeared, the best of these being Gardner & Sons of Manchester, who emerged as a world leader in commercial diesels and exported throughout the world. Their engines powered many British-made trucks and buses throughout the 1950s, '60s and '70s including Bristol and National Buses.

While Gardner's were reliable engines they did not move with the times, particularly in not offering turbocharging units. Truck and bus manufacturers started to look elsewhere and Rolls-Royce and Cummins – the latter opened a factory in Shotts, Lanarkshire – began to pick up Gardner's clients. Glasgow's Albion Motors also used Gardner diesels as well as producing their own, but they too were losing out to other lorry manufacturers incorporating alternative engines. For instance, James Fulton (Junior) Ltd, a Glasgow potato merchants, had had a 100 per cent Albion fleet until the all-conquering Bedford TK came along. The Bedford TK, using Leyland, Perkins and Bedford diesels, was recognisable in many guises, not only as a general purpose lorry but as a chassis for fire engines, Post Office and railway vehicles, as well as military use. The TK and similar engines precipitated the growth of larger and larger lorries and ended the days of petrol engines in any large vehicle. At the time of writing we are in difficulties with the cost of fuel and as high prices at the pump are translated into high prices in the shops, we are having to look more energetically at alternatives.

There are those who might remember electric milk floats, commonly used throughout Britain. Between the wars several manufacturers were producing these and they came into their own during the Second World War as petrol was rationed. Smaller electric vehicles were commonly used within factories and seated trolleys were certainly used to convey visitors around the Empire Exhibition at Bellahouston Park in 1938. I also remember electric dustbin lorries of a substantial size on the streets of Glasgow. Now we are coming full circle as at least one British company is exchanging diesel engines in dustbin lorries for electric ones, the cost being much cheaper than new ones. In fact, it was the cost which stopped the early expansion of electric vehicles as resources were poured into the diesel engine at a time when most people were untroubled by the environmental costs of extracting oil, or climate change.

However, as battery technology has developed substantially we may see an accelerated move towards electric lorries as many manufacturers are responding to customers' needs and a number of supermarkets are beginning to use them. The key to success may be the availability of fast-charging points. Already it has been shown that electric delivery lorries can be on the road for long periods if they can charge up while they are delivering goods.

We already discovered that Aberdeen has pioneered the use of hydrogen fuel cells in its fleet of buses. The City Council there has also embarked on a plan to make the city a centre of excellence for hydrogen technology by using its existing skills in oil and gas to develop hydrogen projects. Besides buses it now has hydrogen-powered vans, road sweepers and waste trucks.

Meanwhile, in another quite exciting development, Scotland has its first electric fire engine, the world's first. Commissioned by Scottish Fire and Rescue Service and built in Cumnock in Ayrshire by Emergency One, it was launched in October 2020. The E1 EVO uses battery power both for the engine and for the pumps. It will start its working life at Clydesmill in Cambuslang. It is a far cry from the horse-drawn fire engines first seen in Glasgow, but then again, we have always been innovative in firefighting. We have had to be, given that Glasgow was once called 'Tinderbox City' due to the high number of fires.

Glasgow was the first brigade in Great Britain to introduce, in 1903, a motorised turntable ladder and, much later, the 'Scoosher', a fire appliance that incorporated a hydraulic boom with a heat detector and a steel spike to break windows. A jet of water would then be sent through the window, all by remote control. It was introduced in 1968 to work in the confines of Glasgow's warehouse and tenement lanes.

Scania P280 fire tender based at Calton Fire Station, on Argyle Street. (Michael Meighan)

Motoring – The Car Age

While cars had been manufactured in Scotland, particularly in Glasgow with the Argyll and the Albion, these were in relatively small numbers and tended to be coach-built high-end vehicles. By 1932 when the Scottish Motor Show was held at the Kelvin Hall, virtually all cars were from England and Europe. This was the beginning of a mass market in family and touring cars with the Wolseley Sixteen appearing on the front page of *The Motor* in November of that year.

Also appearing at the exhibition were the Standard Little Nine, the Vauxhall Cadet, the Armstrong Siddeley and the Morris Oxford, the Hillman Minx, all marques that have disappeared in the exhausts of time.

While there were no Scottish cars, there were a number of large Scottish dealers including Thomas Laurie & Co., Taggarts, Prossers and Arnold Clark. Andersons of Newton Mearns presented the Hillman Hunter and is shown here advertising the Hillman Super Minx in the 1960s. It ceased trading in 1980. Harry Prosser's company, last trading from Royston Road, was a main dealer for Wolseley and at one time converted Wolseley chassis into ambulances. Harry was also instrumental in forming the Scottish Motor Trades Association.

Perhaps the best-known name in the motor trade in Scotland is Arnold Clark. Just like my father, he was a motor mechanic in the services during the Second World War and on demob started by repairing and selling used cars. He opened his first showroom in Park Road, Glasgow, in 1954. This eventually turned into Scotland's largest private business. Arnold Clark sponsors the international four-team invitation football trophy, the Arnold Clark Cup. It was last held in February 2023 with the final in Bristol, where England beat South Korea 4–0 to take the trophy for the second year running.

Car registration plates were one of the many regulations given to us by the 1930 Road Traffic Act and my memories of cars start at this point in the 1950s when I was a young boy collecting the registration numbers, which you could do given there were so few cars around, as proven by the Morris Minor seen in a very empty and cobbled Union Street.

The Morris Minor was considered to be one of the first modern cars. It was first introduced in 1948 and between then and 1971 over 1.3 million were produced. The first, the MM, was produced from 1948 to 1953 and the Series II from 1952 to 1956. The last, the 1000, was produced from 1965 to 1971.

THE SCOTTISH SHOW—Illustrated Report

4D

The Motor

THE NEW **WOLSELEY** SIXTEEN
£325

"THE MOST ADVANCED CAR OF THE YEAR,
WITH THE SIMPLEST GEAR CHANGE OF ALL."

WOLSELEY MOTORS (1927) LTD.
WARD END, BIRMINGHAM.

The Motor at the Scottish Motor Show at Kelvin Hall in 1932. (Michael Meighan Collection)

Andersons of Newton Mearns Hillman Super Minx advertised in the 1960s.

At Charing Cross two very sporty cars occupy the road while ladies in cloche hats wait to cross. It must be the 'Roaring Twenties'. (Michael Meighan Collection)

In Union Street with a Morris Minor 1000. The owner has maybe popped into John Collier's 'The window to watch', for a new suit. (James Meighan Collection)

I can still remember our very first car, a later version Ford Consul, registration GSN 820. It was only the second car in the close, the first being Freddy Thomson's Triumph Mayflower. Our car wasn't new because we were not that posh. It was actually bought from the auction mart that took place in the cattle market in the Gallowgate when the cattle weren't there – but the smells were. I remember my father showing me the wooden machine at the Gallowgate that came down over a 'coo's' neck in order to stun it before death. He promptly pulled my head back out before I did something stupid; this was, of course, before foot-and-mouth, and people and beasts could freely mingle.

The vehicles on display were wide and varied, ranging from ex-police Ford Consuls and Zephyrs as well as old buses and military vehicles. It was brilliant to be able to climb in and out of them and watch them all being started up to test before the auction. I wasn't at the auction when our car was bought, but my father turned up with the said Consul and there was nothing for it but to go for a wee run 'doon the water'.

While police and other public service cars were required to be from British manufacturers, following the Second World War there were many imported cars. Perhaps the most numerous were from Renault, which gave us the small and elegant Dauphine, and we had a later version of the boxy Renault 4. Renault continues to be a popular marque and we are very familiar with the clever marketing of the Clio. We were quite loyal to Renault over the years, buying the brand-new Scenic, one of the first in Scotland.

At Charing Cross a broken-down Austin A40 Devon is being pushed along by an unfortunate driver. Ibrox will have to wait. (Michael Meighan Collection)

A last 2CV hiding in the 'Hidden Lane' off Dumbarton Road. (Michael Meighan Collection)

Another French car is the familiar Citroën 2CV, which was launched in 1953 and considered by *Autocar* to be the most original design since the Model T Ford. The oil crisis of the 1970s assisted in the popularity of the 2CV and other manufacturers also responded to the crisis with the Volkswagen Polo and the Ford Fiesta.

Thinking back to the cars that I saw in Glasgow in the 1950s and '60s, there were many strange and innovative ones. I used to think it was a bit odd that not long after the Second World War, in the 1950s, I would see a car made by Messerschmitt of Germany, the company responsible for the Messerschmitt BF 109 fighter jet and the BF fighter bomber. The car actually looked like the cockpit of a fighter jet with the wings cut off. It could carry only a driver and a passenger, in tandem, just like the fighter. The reason for this was that, following the war, Messerchmitt was forbidden from making aircraft, so they turned their hand to alternatives, one being the Kabinenroller (cabinscooter) designed by aircraft engineer Fritz Fend.

A similar concept, but entirely different design, was the Bubble Car that was seen often in Glasgow. The Italian Isetta was a microcar with a front opening which hinged forward, allowing entry. So did the attached steering wheel. The window on the front panel was large and rounded and from the unofficial title that was then applied to other microcars.

From East Germany came the Trabant made from 1957 to 1991. It was unusual in that it was among the first cars to having a plastic body. The plastic was produced from recycled cotton waste. The average lifespan of a Trabant was said to be twenty-eight years and I certainly remember them in Glasgow.

One car which was commonly seen throughout the country was the Invacar, a name shortened from 'invalid carriage'. The Invacar was a manually controlled single-seater microcar that was distributed free to disabled drivers throughout the UK. It was easily recognised in its ice-blue-coloured fibreglass shell. The car was produced in its thousands by a number of manufacturers from 1948 until 1977 when, for safety reasons, all government cars were scrapped and the provision was replaced with the Motability scheme, which offers drivers a modified standard car.

Finally, the strangest car I ever saw in Glasgow, and that in my very own North Street, was an Amphicar, an amphibious car that was manufactured in West Germany and marketed from 1961 to 1968 with production stopping in 1968. It was a small open car, a cabriolet, not unlike a Triumph Herald but sat very high with a cut-away lower front. It was powered by twin propellers mounted under the rear bumper. I really would have liked to come up the Clyde in that.

Perhaps the Amphicar was appearing at the Motor Show or travelling to Monte Carlo? It may seem fanciful now but the famous Monte Carlo rally had a starting point in Glasgow, in Blythswood Square. If I remembered, I would make my way up there to see the 'souped-up' and badged sports and saloon cars being waved off from outside the offices of the Royal Scottish Automobile Club (RSAC). The RSAC was established in 1899 to promote 'automobilism' in Scotland, with one of the founder members, Wiiliam Douglas Weir. Weir's of Cathcart was a famous name in Glasgow industry. With numbers down to 1,200 from a high of 8,000, the club building was closed in 2002 and is now the Blythswood Square Hotel. The badge of the RSAC is still on the building and the club still exists as RSAC Motorsport and organises the RSAC Scottish Rally.

Nowadays we are quite used to cars being reliable and, given the amount of vehicles on the road, it is relatively unusual to see cars break down. Back then, cars being pushed along was a common sight. We've also forgotten about the fact that cars often lacked proper heaters, and the radios were quite primitive, if the car had one at all.

Before the syncromesh gear, drivers had to go through a complicated business of double-declutching, which is putting the gearstick in neutral before pushing the clutch and then engaging the next gear in order to move forward. Otherwise they would 'crunch the gears' and the gearbox would end up full of little bits of broken metal.

Just imagine on a cold morning trying to defrost the car. The windscreen would be frozen and with no de-icer, scraping would be the only option. While you can still buy them, snow chains used to be seen often on cars. While city centre roads would be kept clear of ice, it would be virtually impossible to travel any distance on ordinary tyres on thick snow, or ice. Chains would be wrapped around the wheels and this would give a better grip. They were cold and messy to attach and you had better not forget they were on when the snow cleared, as you would damage the tyres. The other issue would be starting, particularly in the cold. Even into the early 1960s many cars would have to be started with a starter handle – a long crank that would be inserted into a hole in the front grille and would be used to turn over the engine. It put many a shoulder out.

Cars also had a 'choke', which was a knob on the dashboard connected to the carburettor. This controlled the flow of petrol to the engine, but you had to be careful not to give it too much choke or the carburettor would flood and you would be stuck until it dried out.

As time went by most of these difficulties were ironed out. The advances to cars are endless and we now wonder how we managed without adjustable heated seats, electric windows, sat navs, electronic keys, automatic braking and a host of other improvements. Our chosen service centres will also tell us when we need a service. The tax authorities also know if we have not paid our car tax; we don't need an old-fashioned tax disc on our windscreen anymore.

We have come a long way since the Wolseley Sixteen at the Motor Show in the Kelvin Hall in 1932. Gone are the days of a multitude of manufacturers with a wide variety of designs. While 'concept cars' may be produced, car design is now fairly standard among most companies. Cars look much the same, and often contain identical components. As we move slowly towards cleaner and greener electric cars, we will be moving away from petrol and diesel, and that will see many changes. I say 'slowly' quite deliberately as industry has indeed been very slow to adopt electric cars. From 1900 to the 1950s a number of manufacturers were successfully building electric vehicles that competed well with the internal combustion engine. However, the improvement in road infrastructure, the increasing availability of petroleum, mass manufacturing techniques as well as the continuing improvements in car technology such as the electric starter made the petrol car cheaper.

The tables are turning as improvements in battery technology now make driving longer distances possible. Electric car charging points are also more and more available. As our understanding of global warming and its effects on our environment improves, so does the demand for change and more people are now moving to electric vehicles.

Signs for safety advertising the North British Rubber Company's tyres. (Michael Meighan Collection)

Fast Blacks and Jo Baxi's – The Glasgow Taxi

In the batch of magic lantern slides I got some time ago the one with the noble chap was marked 'first cab driver'. I am presuming this means the first cab driver in Partick as the photos are all from there. What an elegant top hat.

The black taxi cab, 'Fast Black' or 'Joe Baxi', is a very familiar sight in Glasgow and as a wee boy I remember that the Glasgow Taxi Owners Association (TOA) had a stand at exhibitions in Glasgow, probably the Modern Home Exhibition, and they would happily hand out folding cardboard hats to children. It was quite a clever way of promoting the cabs.

Glasgow's first cab driver – probably Partick. (Michael Meighan Collection)

Cabs at George Square with the Merchants Building behind, by George Washington Wilson. (Michael Meighan Collection)

Just like buses, taxicabs would have originally been introduced by local entrepreneurs taking advantage of the growth in travel into and around the city. Just like the beginnings of buses, it looks like the same competition and crowding attended the beginnings of the trade. Parliament, in 1654, acted to implement an ordinance for the Regulation of Hackney Coachmen in London and places adjacent. This was followed by the first licences issued in London in 1662 and applied to horse-drawn vehicles for hire. While there is some doubt about the derivation of the title Hackney carriage, it is thought that this came from the Hackney area of London, although an alternative is that it is derived from the French *hacquenée*, meaning a horse for hire.

Often these would be private coaches with the owners' crests painted over, but as the trade developed, specific vehicles were built. One of these was the Hansom cab designed by Joseph Hansom, an architect from York (cab being short for cabriolet, a light horse-drawn carriage developed in France). With the introduction of taximeters to price fares, the name became taxicab, and then reduced to taxi.

In the photographs here, the two-wheeled vehicles will be Hansom cabs while the four-wheeled version was called a 'growler', a nickname for a second-hand Clarence, a coach named after the Duke of Clarence, later King William IV.

As the petrol engine revolutionised car travel, it did the same for the taxi trade. The first motor taxis simply used what was available, very often Renaults, 500 of which revolutionised the business. There were others including Humber, Wolseley-Siddeley, Napier, Panhard and Glasgow's own Argyll.

It wasn't until another Glasgow company introduced a cab designed specifically for the market that taxis took on a new look. William Beardmore and Company was best known for battleships, naval guns and airships but moved into vehicle manufacturing following the end of the First World War. In 1919 they introduced a new taxi with a 1,486 cc four-cylinder 11.4. It was produced in Anniesland and introduced at Olympia in 1919. Various versions of the cab were then produced in Anniesland, Paisley and Coatbridge. The taxi and its variants proved to be sturdy vehicles, meeting strict requirements set by the Metropolitan Police.

The taxi became extremely popular and through mergers and takeovers the cab existed in various versions until final production of the Mk7 Paramount in 1966. By that time, competition was growing, particularly from the Austin 12/4 which dominated the market until the 1970s.

Another name particularly associated with what became known as the London taxicab was Mann and Overton, who had been dealers for the French-made Unic cab. With rising costs they explored other manufacturers and agreed with Austin to modify an existing vehicle. The first High Lot (or Upright Grand) was soon outselling Beardmore's and the other competitor, Morris Commercial.

St Enoch Square in the 1930s with Austin taxis. No. 5 is going to Croftfoot, the terminus before Castlemilk was built. (Michael Meighan Collection)

1940s. Beyond the tram is the taxi rank at Central station. The iconic sign was changed to 'Outgoing vehicles only'. (Michael Meighan Collection)

Taxis were first regulated in London in 1654, and some form of regulation has applied to taxis in Great Britain ever since, and this has generally been controlled by local authorities, in Glasgow by the City Council where the Licensing and Regulatory Committee controls taxis and private hire owners as well as booking offices. The conditions for a licence include a topographical test, 'the Knowledge', which examines prospective taxi drivers on how well they know the city including layout and landmarks.

Ever since 1945, in a time of austerity after the Second World War, thousands of taxi drivers throughout Glasgow have organised and taken part in the annual 'Outing to Troon', which sees the drivers in fancy dress and decorated cabs take children 'doon the water' for a fantastic day out in Troon. The outing was originated by three drivers, R. McLaren, J. Sampson and W. Campbell, who organised a successful bus run in 1945. As they had some cash leftover, they decided to give some invalid children a day at the seaside. From Eastpark home they convoyed in taxis to Saltcoats. Billy McGregor and the Gaybirds, a popular band at the Glasgow Barrowland, entertained and became a fixture until the mid-1950s.

Nowadays, the black cab competes with ride-hailing cabs and while many traditional cab drivers and companies were slow to adapt to the technology and apps, many have now done so.

By the way, in case you were wondering, Joe Baksi was an American heavyweight boxer who visited Great Britain in the 1940s. He must have taken a taxi.

An Austin FX4 heads up the Saltmarket and waits at the lights at Glasgow Cross while a 'red bus' to Anderston Cross bus station turns down to travel along the Broomielaw. (Michael Meighan Collection)

Glasgow's Changing Streets and Roads

If you had been standing halfway up what is now Glasgow's High Street in 1350, just as the Black Death hit the town, you would have seen above you the imposing Glasgow Cathedral, and below, the mixed stone and wood houses leading down to the river. Away to the west and to the east, you would see the rigs or furrows cultivated by the residents for their own use, and for selling. You might see cottages stretching up towards Cowcaddens, and the occasional big house. People may be travelling on foot or on ponies. The population would be around 1,500 at this time and was growing slowly but haphazardly, bearing in mind that there was no such thing as a town planner.

With the demolition of the West Port and expansion westwards around 1750, Glasgow emerged from the medieval age. At that time, it consisted of four main streets: Saltmarket, Gallowgate, Trongate, and the High Street leading up to the cathedral.

It looks like tarmacadam on Buchanan Street. It must be one of the first streets to be laid with it. (Michael Meighan Collection)

It was around 1764 that the town began to be formally planned by James Barrie, Glasgow's first 'surveyor and measurer'. His survey formed the basis for future building as the town expanded along the main streets, the back areas of which had been rigs – narrow fields. The new developments followed these to form an area that now includes Jamaica Street and Queen Street. In 1772, the new grid system started above Ingram Street and was further extended westwards by James Craig, who was responsible for the original plans for Blythswood Square and the surrounding area of Georgian houses.

As trade and industry grew, the city of Glasgow continued its expansion following the river downstream as the foundries, factories, workshops and shipyards grew on the banks.

In time, the existing villages and estates surrounding Glasgow were consumed to become wards of the city. My own Anderston was one of those independent villages. The lands had been given to the Bishop of Glasgow by King James II of Scotland in 1450, remembered by the still existing Bishop Street, where I went to school. Named after James Anderson of Stobcross House, Anderston changed from farmlands to weaving cottages, bleaching and dyeing greens and then became a major cotton centre. In the process it swallowed up the estates of Lancefield and Hydepark. As the river was deepened and enlarged, it was to become an area of warehousing, whisky bonds and factories. Some areas with pretentions of remaining desirable suburbs, like Finnieston and Dennistoun, were also overwhelmed by industrial buildings and low-cost tenements.

Trongate in Edwardian times. (Michael Meighan Collection)

It was inevitable that moving around the city would become more and more difficult as factories and yards grew as close to the river as they could, for this was the main entry and export point to Scotland for goods from throughout the world. The streets around the river were congested. While the city was indeed growing on a planned grid system, the capacity of the roads was limited.

You can possibly imagine the growing chaos caused by thousands of horses and carts making their way through the city and also waiting for entrance to the docks to collect or offload. This congestion was one of the gripes of the early carters who were paid by the number or journeys they undertook and nothing for waiting time.

You probably couldn't imagine the smell of horse and ordure, and the noise as heavy carts clattered over the cobbles. When it rained it would be appalling and the poor carters were unprotected from the weather.

Tarmacadam, a road covering of crushed stone mixed with sand and tar, began to be applied to roads around the early 1900s and this made a huge difference to the progress of carts along the city streets.

The development of passenger transport also helped with the Cluthas, trams and railways speeding citizens on their way to and from work, but change was very slow and the city had to live with heavy traffic through the age of the horse and cart and even heavy lorries and steam engines, some of them pulling locomotives and machinery and even huge guns through the busy streets from works at Springburn and Parkhead. You might also imagine the effect on the environment as all this combined with smoke from industrial fires and furnaces, as well as railways, to produce a seething cauldron of poison that people had to live in.

As always, there were other priorities. While the City Council was able to boast wide avenues and leafy council garden estates from the 1920s, two wars got in the way of any kind of general improvement in traffic conditions and it was to remain much the same into the 1960s. That did not mean that plans for redevelopment were not being considered.

Glasgow throughout most of the early twentieth century was not an attractive place to live, but plans were afoot to do something about it. The Bruce Report was the starting point.

In 1945 the Bruce Report was published by City Engineer and Master of Works Robert Bruce. Officially called *The First Planning Report to the Highways and Planning Committee of the Corporation of the City of Glasgow*, the main thrust was to redevelop the city within its existing boundaries, building up rather than out as there was actually very little space for expansion within the city boundary. However, there was an alternative report produced by the government in 1949: the *Clyde Valley Regional Plan*. This advocated relocation as a policy and in particular the movement of citizens to the new towns of East Kilbride, Cumbernauld and further afield. This was seen by Glasgow councilors as gerrymandering; a means whereby the strong Labour support within the city could be dispersed and diminished. However, parts of both reports were accepted and redevelopment started, leading to two decades of demolition and building in and around the city.

No. 28 Saltmarket by Thomas Annan, around 1870. (Michael Meighan Collection)

It was a period of intensive activity and a bonanza for contractors and haulage companies. While streams of lorries carried rubble out of town to landfill, work started on the new towns and 'schemes'. These included Castlemilk, Drumchapel, Easterhouse, Pollock and the Red Road flats in Balornock. Glasgow acquired more high-rise buildings than any other city in Europe and also became the biggest landlord.

Glaswegians will be familiar with the M8 and the Kingston Bridge, as well as the M74. I would certainly take exception to the fact that we were moved from our 'slum' tenement to make way for the Kingston Bridge, for our building was far from being a slum and was equal to many of the buildings still standing and since renovated in Anderston and Partick. We even had an inside toilet and a bath! Our house certainly wasn't big enough for a family with four boys and the move was our chance for a new start away from the smog of the inner city.

Still, the M8 was built and we were moved. While the building of the motorway through Townhead, Anderston, Cowcaddens, Kingston, Tradeston and Govan did mean the removal of much of Glasgow's poor housing, it also meant the removal of many fine buildings, particularly at Charing Cross, including the whole east side of my own North Street. What is not realised is that the M8 through these areas and the M74 in the south and east was only part of what was to be an inner ring road; this road was to go through many of the 'leafy' parts of Glasgow. There was such an outcry that the rest of the Inner Ring Road Initiative was shelved. This included a motorway through Maryhill and north to Balloch! It has taken forty years for the completion of the link from the M8 to the M74 and while not the exact route suggested by Bruce, the link is now there.

Bridges

Integral to the new motorway system was the crossing of what had always been the cause of traffic bottlenecks: the River Clyde. This was achieved in the building of the Kingston Bridge that takes the M8 from Anderston to Kingston on the Southside. Until the building of the Erskine Bridge, it was possibly the largest link over the Clyde. This and the many other crossings of the Clyde, the Kelvin and other smaller rivers reflects the growing city and its economic prosperity.

It is known that a wooden bridge crossed the Clyde in 1345 at what is now Stockwell Street (a stock being a tree trunk or post, presumably where there was a well). At the time this would have been the lowest crossing point on the river and here the wooden bridge was replaced around 1410 with an eight-arched stone bridge to link Glasgow to the growing Gorbals.

This remained the only bridge until 1772 when the Broomielaw, now called Glasgow Bridge, was opened. It was designed by William Mylne and civil engineer John Smeaton. As it sits at the bottom of Jamaica Street it became known informally as the Jamaica Bridge. It was replaced in 1836 by Thomas Telford and again between 1895 and 1899, incorporating Telford's original stone but expanding the arches to allow for larger ships.

On the other side of the Caledonian Railway Bridge is the George V Bridge. It may look as traditional as the Jamaica Bridge but is years ahead in terms of technology. While the

Jamaica Bridge was built of stone blocks, the three-arched George V Bridge was built of reinforced concrete box girders with a facing of Dalbeattie granite. It was designed by City Engineer Thomas Somers.

The bridge links the city to Tradeston on the south. While it was commissioned in 1914, the First World War prevented its completion. This was achieved in 1928, giving improved access to the city's docks and relieving pressure on the Jamaica Bridge. It also allowed for higher loads to cross the river as there was little headroom on the streets leading off Eglinton Street, underneath the railway above, to allow traffic to pass under.

There had been, and continues to be, accidents when high loads hit the bridges above. In September 1994 three young Girl Guides from Drumchapel and two Guide leaders were killed when a double-decker bus hit the bridge in Cook Street.

While the George V Bridge relieved some of the traffic congestion, there continued to be a need for improved communications across and through the city. This was recognised in the Bruce Report discussed earlier. Part of this was the construction of an inner ring road. This was the M8 motorway that would run round the city from Townhead destroying much of Charing Cross and Anderston, crossing the river on the Kingston Bridge and taking traffic to the south and Glasgow Airport.

While at 180-metre clearance the bridge seems very high, apparently the river authorities insisted on the height to allow river dredgers upstream to the George V Bridge. With hindsight this seems to have been nonsense as river traffic was decreasing quickly. River steamers no longer left the Broomielaw and there were few coasters offloading.

The bridge had first been proposed in 1945 and construction work started in 1967. William Fairhurst was the consulting engineer and the construction was a joint venture between Marples Ridgway and Willie Logan. My first job after school was with Willie Logan, building the tunnels under the motorway taking surface water down to the Clyde.

The bridge was opened in 1970 by Queen Elizabeth the Queen Mother. The bridge is named after the Southside area where it lands, Kingston, its name being another reminder of the sugar, rum and slave trade between Glasgow and the Caribbean. In order to accommodate the bridge on the south, Glasgow's first enclosed harbour, the Kingston Dock, was closed to shipping and filled in. On the north side, in order to accommodate the on-ramps to the bridge, me and my family were relocated to the leafy suburbs.

The bridge was designed to handle 120,000 vehicles but by 1990 defects in design and construction, and unpredicted growth in traffic size and weight, were causing problems.

The remedial work turned out to be one of Glasgow's largest civil engineering projects. It involved lifting the 52,000-ton deck by using 128 hydraulic jacks and lowering it down to new supporting piers, all while traffic was still moving! It is recorded in the Guinness Book of Records as the biggest bridge lift ever. The bridge now handles 150,000 vehicles per day and 'Traffic is slow on the Kingston Bridge' is a common radio traffic report.

With the continuing development of the City of Glasgow, particularly Pacific Quay and the Glasgow Science Centre on the Southside at Govan and in Finnieston with the Clyde Auditorium and the Scottish Exhibition and Conference Centre (SEC), a new bridge was required to link these major developments, as well as generally open up the areas under the Kingston Bridge and the ongoing developments along the south shore of the Clyde. The off ramp emerging at Kingston caused problems to local traffic.

The Kingston Bridge. (Michael Meighan Collection)

The 'Squinty Bridge' was one of the solutions. The bridge being in Glasgow, you probably know already that this would not be its real name. Its given name is the Clyde Arc, and it was designed in a shape whereby the supporting structure starts on one side at one end and ends on the opposite side. The bridge was designed by Halcrow and built by Edmund Nutall, completed in April 2006. Although it is designed to have a lifespan

Entry to the M8 at Anderston with the fenced-off 'road to nowhere' above. It's open now. (Michael Meighan)

of 120 years, it has had a difficult beginning with one of the fourteen supporting cables snapping. On inspection further stress faults were detected, resulting in the bridge being closed for six months.

The bridge is designed to take four traffic lanes but two of these are confined to public transport only with the possibility in the future that it may be used for a tramway.

Once again, Glaswegians have shown their love of renaming structures. No exception is the Tradeston Bridge, a pedestrian and cycling bridge built between International Financial Services District (IFSD) in Anderston and Tradeston on the south bank. It has been named the Squiggly Bridge as it is constructed in an 'S' shape to give it enough length to allow clearance for boats while not making it too steep.

This is not the only pedestrian bridge and certainly not a new idea. That belongs back to when thousands would make their way over the river from the Gorbals, Kinning Park and beyond to work in the mills and factories in Bridgeton and Barrowfield. In the other direction was the huge bakery of the United Cooperative Baking Society in McNeill Street and the Govan Iron Works – the famous Dixon's Blazes at Govanhill.

This crossing is the St Andrew's Bridge, an elegant wrought-iron structure spanning the Clyde in front of the home of the Glasgow Humane Society on the Glasgow Green, close to the People's Palace museum. The bridge was built to replace a busy ferry at the same place. The cast-iron Corinthian columns support flat chain links to which are attached the lattice girder single span. It was built by Glasgow engineer Neil Robson between 1853 and 1855. The contractor was P. and W. McLellan, bridge builders and engineers at the Clutha works, Florence Street, Gorbals.

The other suspension bridge is the South Portland Street Suspension Bridge that links the city to Laurieston and Gorbals. It was built a couple of years before the St Andrew's Bridge, replacing a wooden bridge on the site. This deck is supported at either end by arched sandstone towers. It doesn't have a very exciting name and if they were ever asked, Glaswegians might not know even what it is called.

There is also the pedestrian Bell's Bridge built for the Glasgow Garden Festival in 1988 to allow passage from the exhibition area over to the Scottish Exhibition and Conference Centre and rail access.

With the continued developments on either side of the river, new bridges continue to be built and I look forward to another being constructed between Water Row in Govan and

St Andrew's suspension bridge in the Glasgow Green. (Michael Meighan)

the Riverside Museum area. This promises to assist in reinvigorating Govan by linking the new 'West End Innovation Quarter' around Glasgow University to mixed housing and commercial space across the river in Govan.

Tunnels

Commonly known as the Finnieston Tunnel, the Glasgow Harbour Tunnel at No. 28 Tunnel Street was completed in 1895 by the Glasgow Harbour Tunnel Company for vehicular and passenger traffic under the harbour of Glasgow between Finnieston and Mavisbank.

There were three 16-foot-diameter tunnels, one for pedestrians and two for vehicles. While pedestrians would walk down several flights to reach the tunnel, vehicles would be lowered on hydraulic lifts. These stairs and lifts, provided by the Otis Elevator Company of New York, were contained within the North and South Rotundas. Designed by Simpson and Wilson, these iconic buildings remain as memorials to Glasgow's transport

The North Rotunda of the Glasgow Harbour Tunnel showing where the vehicles entered. (Michael Meighan)

and industrial past. The South Rotunda was a central feature of the famous Glasgow Garden Festival in 1988, hosting a replica of Nardini's famous ice-cream parlour in Largs. It has since been restored and converted to offices. The North Rotunda is now a restaurant and wedding venue.

While the original prospectus contained a clause to the effect that the Corporation of Glasgow and the police commissioners of Govan might acquire the tunnels after fourteen years, the enterprise did not last that long. On 30 April 1907, the tunnels were in trouble. The trustees of the Clyde Navigation had introduced the Finnieston, a vehicle ferry, virtually above the tunnel and the tunnel could not compete with the lower tolls on the ferry. The tunnels were closed to save the shareholders from further losses.

The tunnels were reopened in 1912 and from 1915 Glasgow Corporation gave an annual grant until they were bought by the Corporation in 1926. The vehicle tunnels were closed in 1943 and the metal removed. Memory is fickle but I do remember my father telling me that he certainly drove lorries through it during his career with a removals company in the 1940s. Originally the traffic was horses and carts. I assumed that this might scare horses but a report said that they took to the tunnels well and as the carters could avoid the steep inclines onto the vehicle ferries, they could carry extra loads. The pedestrian tunnel was reopened in 1940. Before the final closure in the 1980s, as a wee boy, I used the tunnel often on my adventures around the docks. Back then the tunnel was a spooky place. Through the entrance door you went down broad timber stairs to a booth where at one time you would buy a ticket. Continuing down, the stairs were contained within quite high timber walls and it was very difficult to see over, down to the abandoned vehicle tunnels. You could certainly hear the drips, if not cascade, of water falling below. The pedestrian tunnel was a dark and gloomy place as it was badly lit. You also shared the walkway with a large-diameter water main. It was also not a very busy place and rarely would you meet others using the tunnel. Car use, the availability of the pedestrian ferries and reduced industrial activity on the South Side led to closure in 1980 and the long-neglected vehicle tunnels were sealed in 1986.

The Clyde Tunnel

Before the Second World War and before there were any plans for the Clyde Tunnel, Glasgow Corporation had been considering a high-level bridge at Finnieston. With the outbreak of the war, those plans were shelved in favour of a complete rethink of transport in and around the city. The Clyde Tunnel was the answer; it would allow traffic to bypass the city centre if it didn't need to be there. A survey at the time concluded that 25 per cent of the traffic crossing the George V Bridge, then the lowest crossing point, was travelling from north-west to south-west. A new crossing would immediately relieve congestion in the city centre. The new tunnel would also eventually be part of the planned outer ring road in the Bruce Report. While the tunnel was planned just after the Second World War, it was not started until 1957.

It was built using a system in which water and mud was prevented from seeping in by using compressed air. The miners would enter the tunnel through air locks and use a shield at the tunnel head where the silt and rock would be excavated. The shield, the same diameter as the tunnel, 29 feet, was pushed forward on hydraulic rams as the miners excavated rock and sand, which was taken away on a conveyer belt, just like coal in a mine.

Unlike the Glasgow Harbour Tunnel, the Clyde Tunnel answered the call of the motor car and provided substantial access roads on both sides of the river. As we now know, some of the plans for a ring of motorways round the city did not come to fruition. The idea was that tunnel traffic would be able to immediately access motorways on both banks of the river. If you lived in Anniesland as I did then, you will know that the tunnel basically emerges east and west straight onto Dumbarton Road and north onto Crow Road, which after a desultory dual carriageway becomes a normal city road before it hits Anniesland Cross and then onto the Switchback Road. That was all intended to become a motorway but thankfully it was part of the rethink that stopped the continued destruction of the fine buildings of the city.

This rethink also stopped Dumbarton Road from becoming a dual carriageway, instead, channeling traffic along a widened Victoria Drive, as it is today.

Service buses run through the tunnel now but it seems silly to us today that Glasgow Corporation originally decided not to run them through the tunnel for fear that they would provide competition for the Subway.

What Might Have Been

We know that the Scots were an inventive nation, with products of that invention travelling the world. James Watt, William Murdoch, Alexander Fleming, John Scott Russell and James 'Paraffin' Young have all made their mark. In road transport John Loudon McAdam gave us Macadamised roads. Kirkpatrick Macmillan and/or Thomas McCall gave us the bicycle and Robert William Thomson and John Boyd Dunlop gave the pneumatic tyre. David Dunbar Buick gave us the overhead valve engine.

Perhaps one of the strangest inventions was Bennie's Railplane. George Bennie was an inventive Glaswegian from an engineering family who, in 1923, was granted a patent for a 'Railplane', a high-level suspended monorail system over the LNER siding at Burnbrae Dyeworks at Milngavie. The idea was that passenger traffic could travel at high speed above the slow-moving freight travelling below. The design for the electrically powered Railplane was by engineer Hugh Fraser and it was built by William Beardmore & Co., famous for airships and battleships.

Despite initial enthusiasm after the launch in 1930, all but media interest waned in the project that might have seen Railplanes travelling in Great Britain, the Middle East and Europe. They were unable to get financial backing and Bennie was ousted from the company in 1936, being declared bankrupt in 1937. The Railplane was sold for scrap in 1956 and Bennie died in 1957. The Railplane concept has always fascinated new generations of Glaswegians, wondering what might have been.

Above: 'Railplane', a high-level suspended monorail system over the LNER siding at Burnbrae Dyeworks at Milngavie. (Michael Meighan Collection)

Right: Inside the Bennie Railcar. (Michael Meighan Collection)

And What Might Be?

As I come to the end of this book, we see a very different Glasgow from how it was during its industrial heyday. Gone are virtually all of the shipyards, as are the many busy docks from which ships of all nations berthed to unload produce and from where we sent goods around the world. King George V Dock is now the only dock for oceangoing vessels on the Upper Clyde. Produce now goes directly by lorry or by train from rail or sea terminals in other parts of the UK. Instead, where there once were cranes and warehouses there are now offices and flats, as well as the Scottish Exhibition and Conference Centre, the Riverside Museum and the Science Centre, with many more new developments to come.

These huge improvements, along the banks of the Clyde within the city, have allowed walking and cycling routes. The redeveloped Subway promises to make that an even more popular transport option, as does the prospect of new railway stations and links.

At the time of writing we have been emerging from the worldwide threat of Covid-19 and the restrictions that we have had to live under. We are now in difficult times living not with the threat of a pandemic but of potential shortages of fuel and food supplies. It has made us begin to think seriously about our greener transport future.

All stop for the start of Great Scottish Run in Glasgow. (Michael Meighan Collection)

While I was an avid cyclist in my youth, except for the suburbs and wealthier areas, the inner city was never conducive to the bike. However, you did see delivery bikes with a large basket at the front to carry products such as butcher's meat or groceries. For the tenement dweller security was a problem, as was storage; sometimes I would see bikes suspended from the ceiling in peoples' hallways. I didn't have that problem. As a boy I would get my bike from our locked rooftop washhouse (unusual in Glasgow), take it downstairs and cycle up North Street and Kelvingrove Park to Park Circus. The joy was cycling down home at speed through the park in the quiet early morning.

I was delighted to learn that my route is now part of the West City Way, one of a number of new cycle routes through the city. From Anderston to Kelvingrove it uses the 'Bridge to nowhere'. There were a few of these peculiar remnants when some projects during the 1960s were left unfinished. The pedestrian bridge was intended to travel over the M8 approach roads in Anderston to the city and to the riverside but never did, until now.

With new developments in electric bikes and readily available charging and bike racks, I hope we can see a more bike-friendly and healthy city. I recently passed a well-known pub in Partick outside which there were two new bike racks. Great, except that they were being leant against by three of the pub's patrons as they enjoyed a pint and a smoke. We need to get past 'The Glasgow Effect': the lower life expectancy of Glasgow residents compared to the rest of Scotland, the UK and European countries. There can be many reasons for this including lifestyle and social conditions but doing something about environmental conditions would surely help. We also need to get over our love affair with the car, and back to public transport and particularly to walking, which Glaswegians used to love. While we know that active and sustainable travel is good for us and for the environment, unfortunately recent surveys have shown that we are going in the wrong direction. Car usage in Glasgow has been increasing, and vehicle emissions continue to increase. We are not walking as much as we used to, but perhaps recent events, and the cost of fuel, will make us think about our health and the health of our children.

Glasgow City Council has just published an Active Travel Strategy that aims to significantly increase more active travel: 'Walking, wheeling and cycling will be the first and natural choice for everyday journeys, for people of all ages and ability, to travel locally to schools, to shops, to work, or to the city centre.' What a great ambition. Looking further into the future, as part of a comprehensive study into mass transport throughout Scotland, the government, in its Strategic Transport Projects Review, has announced forty-five recommendations which include a Clyde Metro that will be part of an improved rapid transport system throughout the greater Glasgow area. It will be a multibillion development over a thirty-year period which aims to better connect more than 1.5 million people to employment, education and health services in and around Glasgow. According to Councillor Susan Aitken, leader of Glasgow City Council, 'A Clyde Metro can help us address the climate emergency by delivering clean and net-zero carbon connectivity, whilst also providing the affordable, sustainable and integrated transport public transport system our citizens deserve'.

The Riverside Museum

I couldn't complete this book without paying tribute to the City of Glasgow, its museum curators and the volunteers and enthusiasts who have dedicated themselves to preserving Glasgow's life and culture, and in particular those who preserve and maintain our transport history.

First among these is Glasgow's Riverside Museum, which sits on the River Clyde exactly from where many a new-built ships sailed off to countries around the world. As a wee boy I would often visit the wonderful collection of ship models gifted by shipowners and builders to the city. These fantastically detailed models were used in the building of the ships and for demonstration purposes. These range from miniature models made by French prisoners during the Napoleonic Wars to the huge models of the RMS *Queen Mary* and HMS *Hood*. When gifted, they were crammed side by side into the ground-floor galleries of the Art Gallery and Museum, the 'Ship Court' and surrounded by zoological and ethnological exhibits.

The closure of Glasgow's tram system brought an unexpected bonus: the availability of a separate home for the ship models and other transport exhibits. From 1964 this was in Glasgow's own Transport Museum in the redundant tram depot in Albert Drive, Coplawhill, south of the river. It also allowed preserved trams, buses and other vehicles their own place.

In 1988, a much-enlarged transport collection moved to a section of the Kelvin Hall and all the time was gaining popularity. Not just tourists but Glaswegians like me were visiting it time and time again. As it grew, it was clear that it needed a purpose-built

Riverside Museum and the Tall Ship *The Glenlee*. (Michael Meighan)

home. The status of one of the greatest of Great Britain's transport collections demanded a building which would suit the purpose and which would adequately welcome the growing numbers of appreciative visitors.

The city did it with style, for what was chosen was as dramatic as it was surprising, and in a most appropriate location, set on the riverbank, where, at A. & J. Inglis shipyard, 500 ships were built over a period of 100 years. The tender for the design of the museum was won by the late Zaha Hadid and engineers Buro Happold.

The building is spectacular and as I watched it being built it was with growing excitement as to what would be the final product. The building doesn't disappoint. Its mountainous facade is reminiscent of Glasgow's history of church and industry. Its huge glass frontage allows ample light to penetrate this mammoth building and also reflects the Tall Ship, *The Glenlee*, anchored in front of it.

The Scottish Maritime Museum in Dumbarton also hosts some great floating exhibits as well as the world-famous Denny Ship Model Experimental Tank used to test the design of hulls by floating models of full-size ships.

The Summerlee Museum of Scottish Industrial Life on the banks of the Monklands Canal and on the remains of the Summerlee Ironworks in Coatbridge includes two Glasgow Corporation trams: a single-decker 'school car' and a Coronation tram built at the Coplawhill works. It's a great family day out and you can even ride on tramcars.

If you would like to see Clydesdale horses at work then you could visit the National Museum of Rural Life in East Kilbride. That too is a great family way to see the work of the farm and how the Clydesdale horse was bred for logging, driving and agriculture. You may even get to ride one.

Finally, I would recommend that you visit the Glasgow Vintage Vehicle Trust housed in the old Corporation bus garage in Bridgeton. Here they have a wonderful collection of public-service and commercial vehicles, some of which you may have seen in this book. Going futher afield, the Scottish Vintage Bus Museum, near Dunfermline, Fife, has over 100 buses as well as trains and a horse tram.

Bibliography

Deayton, Alistair, and Quinn, Iain, *A Macbrayne Album* (Stroud: Amberley Publishing, 2009)

Laird, Ann, *Hyndland: Edwardian Glasgow Tenement Suburb* (Glasgow: Anne Laird, 1997)

McQueen, Andrew, *Clyde River Steamers of the Last Fifty Years* (Glasgow: Gowans and Gray, 1923)

Paul, Robert M., *Partick Anecdotes* (Helensburgh: Jessie Paul and Elizabeth Greer, 1998)

Tuckett, Angela, *The Scottish Carter* (London: George Allen and Unwin Ltd, 1967)

Acknowledgements

I am grateful to all those who have shared their knowledge and images of Glasgow with me. Jane Helen Jones, Bryan Tennant, Alastair Stirling, Roderick Low, Roger Manley and Andy MacDonald for their knowledge of Glasgow buses and trams. Isabel Allison, Bill Farish, Bill McGregor and Merkam Doyle for information on the Maryhill chip van. Bill Mackenzie, Ruxton McDonald and John Mitchell for information on fever ambulances. Derek Smith for his knowledge of cars. John Kemplen and Neil McLuskey for lorries.

As ever, my thanks to Jill for reviewing this work and for her patience and support. I am also grateful to the staff at Amberley Publishing for their support in this and previous works.

Glasgow Cathedral from the Drygate. (Michael Meighan Collection)